Indian Culture *for everyone*

INTACH

Heritage Education and Communication Service, INTACH

ARVIND KUMAR

Sponsored by
The Ministry of Human Resource Development,
Department of Secondary and Higher Education, Government of India
under the scheme 'Strengthening of Culture and Values in Education'

Developed by
Heritage Education and Communication Service
INTACH
71 Lodi Estate, New Delhi 110 003
www.intach.org

Concept, Research, Text:
Heritage Education and Communication Service, INTACH
Shobita Punja
Rohini Kandhari

Design Coordination:
Radha Dayal
Nidhi Gaur

Design, Layout, Illustrations:
Anita Varma

Special thanks to
Center for Cultural Resources and Training, Delhi; Fredrik Arvidsson, and
the Late Jean-Louis Nou, for use of their photographs in this book.

Editor:
Shobita Punja

Copy Editor:
Vandana Mohindra

Published in October 2007 by
Arvind Kumar Publishers
C-1/324, Palam Villas, Palam Vihar
Gurgaon 122017, India
www.arvindkumarpublishers.in

Publishing Chief:
Arundhati Deosthale

Printed by
Vimal Offset, Delhi

ISBN-10: 81-8452-001-8
ISBN-13: 978-81-8452-001-9

Dear Friend,

How does one write a book that explores 10,000 years of history, and bring to it the richness and variety of cultures and communities that live in a country, that is really a subcontinent? How can one attempt to introduce such a complex subject in a simple, yet interesting way?

Indian culture has many facets. One of its distinguishing features lies in the continuity of traditions. Some skills, like pottery, have existed uninterrupted for 5,000 years. Designs on pots from the Harappan civilization of the 3rd millennium BC can still be found on pots made today in Gujarat. The same is true of dance and music, textile making, painting and sculpture.

The arts in India are also integrated and interdependent. A poem about Krishna is part of our written and oral traditions, the subject of performing arts and Indian paintings. Today a woman may use a well-known story of Krishna to decorate her hut wall, the same theme is seen in a three hundred year old Kangra painting preserved in a museum and it also finds expression in dance forms like Kathak in the North, and Bharatnatyam in the South. Artists from different parts of the country have adopted themes and styles, integrating them into the local cultural tradition.

Many of us think that because of our continuous heritage, Indian art and culture is static, and that artists repeated themselves for centuries. This is not true. No two temples look alike, and no two mosques are the same anywhere in this country. This means that the artist-architect took the basic principles of temple or mosque making and created a new form. Similarly, there are over a hundred ways to wear a sari, and each region and every community within it have their own style, weave and colours. This is what makes Indian art absolutely unique – there is always unity in our diversity.

This book offers you kaleidoscopic glimpses of India. Each page has introductory text on top and a timeline below to show you the period that the theme spans. The book has 44 theme based double page spreads and over 200 pictures, drawings, and photographs that are a small sample of what the wonders of India really are.

We urge you to 'read' the pictures; they are clues for what to look for. We hope you enjoy this book and that it opens windows for you to see, understand and appreciate this diverse land, shaped by millions of people, over hundreds of centuries. Join us on this great discovery of India and if you get smitten, as we are, do join INTACH in its efforts to preserve the continuity of this magnificent culture.

Shobita Punja
HECS Team
2007

Contents

The maps in this book are illustrative. They are neither to scale, nor do they accurately reflect the international and state boundaries.

Terracotta elephant

Elephant
The Elephant is widely depicted in Indian art: Indra, the lord of the sky, is shown riding Airavat, an elephant; the Buddha's mother, Maya, dreamt of a white elephant, predicting his birth. Today, Kerala celebrates a festival dedicated to this noble animal.

Tiger, drawn by a child

Tiger
Our national animal has been a symbol of strength and courage since ancient times. In Indian mythology, the tiger is believed to have the power to do everything from fighting demons to creating rain. Sadly, less than 3,000 tigers are left in the wild in India today.

Asiatic Lion
In Indian art, the goddess Durga is depicted as seated on a lion. India's national emblem is taken from Emperor Ashoka's, 3rd century BC, Lion Capital at Sarnath (Uttar Pradesh). Today, India's only wild lions live in Gir National Park in Gujarat.

Goddess Durga astride a lion, miniature painting

Peacock
The god Kartikeya (son of Lord Shiva), rides on a peacock representing elegance and splendour. The peacock, which is India's national bird, is seen as a symbol of immortality because of the annual renewing of its beautiful feathers.

Peacock

Wild Ass

Lion

Elephant

Coral

6

India is a land of great natural beauty and variety. The wonders of nature have inspired and fascinated artists through the ages. Artists watched animals play in the forest, and admired birds as they soared in the sky, and fish as they danced in clear streams.

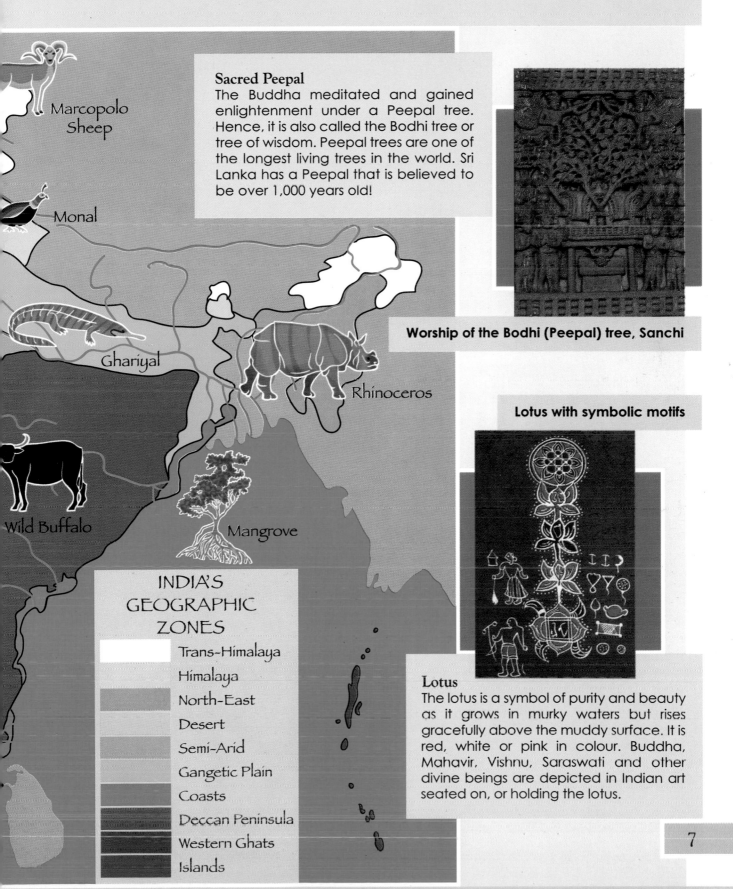

Marcopolo Sheep

Monal

Ghariyal

Rhinoceros

Wild Buffalo

Mangrove

INDIA'S GEOGRAPHIC ZONES

- Trans-Himalaya
- Himalaya
- North-East
- Desert
- Semi-Arid
- Gangetic Plain
- Coasts
- Deccan Peninsula
- Western Ghats
- Islands

Sacred Peepal
The Buddha meditated and gained enlightenment under a Peepal tree. Hence, it is also called the Bodhi tree or tree of wisdom. Peepal trees are one of the longest living trees in the world. Sri Lanka has a Peepal that is believed to be over 1,000 years old!

Worship of the Bodhi (Peepal) tree, Sanchi

Lotus with symbolic motifs

Lotus
The lotus is a symbol of purity and beauty as it grows in murky waters but rises gracefully above the muddy surface. It is red, white or pink in colour. Buddha, Mahavir, Vishnu, Saraswati and other divine beings are depicted in Indian art seated on, or holding the lotus.

7

La Martinier College, Lucknow, U.P.

Architecture

Architecture is the art of designing and constructing buildings. Buildings can be built for specific purposes like a home, an office or a cinema hall. This art requires the knowledge of engineering, mathematics and a sound understanding of natural materials. We say a building is great or beautiful when its shape is pleasing to look at, it is a technological innovation, it uses materials best suited to the environment and its design is functional.

Terracotta sculpture, Mauryan dynasty

Traditional mud houses, Rajasthan

Sculpture

Sculpture is the art of making images out of clay, stone, metal or any other material. Images or sculptures were created for worship at home and in temples, as well as to decorate walls and interiors.

Bronze sculpture of Nataraja, Chola period

The natural world consists of all that nature has given us, while man-made heritage refers to the arts that human societies have created through the ages. There are many types of arts or kala: the performing arts like music and dance, the plastic arts such as architecture, painting and the crafts, as well as the literary arts.

Painting

Painting is the art of applying colour to a background. A painting on cloth is called a textile painting and on a wall it is called a mural painting. Natural colours were derived from leaves and flowers as well as made by grinding semi-precious stones, mud or rocks. The paint was often mixed with a glue to make it stick to the surface or background, and was applied using fingers or a brush. A painting can have a wide range of themes.

Painting by Rabindranath Tagore

Metal toy horse, Central India

Crafts

The arts of India include handicrafts that are made from natural materials and are an important part of our daily life. Great skills are involved in making these crafts that the kalakar or craftsman passes on from one generation to the next, resulting in the continuous growth of crafts over time and historic periods.

Wooden fish, Orissa

Material	Craft
Clay	Pottery, ceramics, toys and utensils
Stone (granite, soapstone, sandstone)	Large sculptures and figurines
Precious and semi-precious stones (gems)	Jewellery
Metal	Jewellery, utensils, sacred images and everyday objects for use in the home
Wood (fragrant sandalwood, hard wood like teak and sal)	Furniture, sculpture, images and figurines
Bamboo	Baskets, hats, mats, plates, umbrellas and other everyday objects
Cotton, silk and wool	Traditional costumes, shawls, blankets and contemporary high-end fashion

3 Performing Arts

DESI FORMS

Music
Each community has its own type of music and tradition of songs. Musicians were patronized with great generosity by kings, queens and other wealthy supporters of the arts. There are essentially two ways to make music: with the human voice, and with an instrument.

Rajasthani Musicians

Dance
There are songs and dances associated with festivals, seasons, work and activities such as harvesting, and with the life-cycle of a human being, such as birth and marriage.

Bhangra, Punjab

Chhau, West Bengal

Theatre
In villages across India, open-air performances — Tamasha in Maharashtra, Nautanki in Himachal Pradesh, Yakshagan in Karnataka, Krishnattam in Kerala and Chhau in Bihar and Bengal are still very popular.

Puppets, Rajasthan

Puppetry
A puppet is a doll or figure representing a person or animal or any object used to tell a story. It can be made of various types of materials that can be moved in various ways.

String puppets from Rajasthan
Glove puppets from Kerala
Rod puppets from Bengal
Shadow puppets from Andhra Pradesh/Orissa

10

From early times, people have expressed emotions and ideas through the performing arts: music, dance, theatre and puppetry. In India there are two branches of art: Margi or the classical forms, and Desi that refers to the arts of several communities across India.

Margi or Classical Indian Music has two styles:
1. Hindustani (from the North)
2. Carnatic (from the South)

Instruments
Instruments can be classified as:
Percussion instruments that produce sound by being struck: cymbals, gongs
Wind instruments that need air to flow through to produce sound: bansuri or flute
String instruments that use strings to create sound: vina, sarod, sitar
Drums made of a membrane stretched across a hollow frame and played by striking: tabla, mridangam

Dance
There are various dance forms in India: classical, regional dance forms from various parts of India, and modern dance.

Theatre
Traditional Indian theatre combines several forms of creative expression such as singing, dancing, miming, painting, designing costumes and masks.

Classical Dance Forms
Bharatnatyam — South India
Kathakali — Kerala
Kathak — North India
Manipuri — Manipur
Odissi — Orissa
Mohiniattam — Kerala
Kuchipudi — Andhra Pradesh

Manipuri dancers

Kuttiyattam
A form of sacred theatre of Kerala, it was originally performed in temple theatres called Kuttampalams of the 12th to 17th centuries by the Chakyar, Nambiar and Nangiar communities. The recitations and the music are classical in character, with an emphasis on hand gestures and eye movements.

This traditional theatre form is in danger of disappearing due to lack of funding to support its productions, and only five of the 18 Chakyar families in the profession remain. UNESCO declared Kuttiyattam an endangered Oral and Intangible Heritage of the World in 2001.

Kuttiyattam, Kerala

11

Shelters and Homes

Shelters, as the name suggests, provide protection from rain, heat and the cold, and from other threats to human safety. A house shelters a family as well as its belongings, and also gives a sense of physical comfort and security.

A stone tool used by Stone Age man

Wall painting, Bhimbetka, M.P.

c.11000 – 7000 BC,
Mesolithic rock art site of Bhimbetka, M.P

2500 BC   2000 BC   1500 BC   1000 BC   500 BC

India, Australia and South Africa have the richest treasures of ancient cave art from the Stone Age period. Early communities that lived over 10,000 years ago made their shelters in natural caves and rock formations in many regions of India. They decorated their homes with paintings, drawings and engravings.

Exterior of caves, Bhimbetka, M.P.

Bhimbetka Discovered
In 1958, while archeologist V.S. Wakankar was travelling by train to Bhopal, he noticed unusual rock formations near Bhimbetka. He returned to the site with a team who then explored these incredible caves.

Wall painting, Bhimbetka, M.P.

World Heritage Site

Bhimbetka, Madhya Pradesh
Bhimbetka is famous for its clusters of natural rock shelters and the paintings that adorn some of these caves. 10,000-year-old flints and stone implements made by hunting and food gathering communities were found here. The paintings depict scenes from everyday life thousands of years ago: hunting scenes, a variety of animals, and representations of celebration, such as people dancing and playing instruments.

To ensure the protection and safe keeping of these caves, Bhimbetka was declared a World Heritage Site by UNESCO in 2004.

Wall painting, Bhimbetka, M.P.

13

500 BC   0   500 AD   1000 AD   1500 AD   2000 AD

Tents as Shelters

Tents are temporary shelters or movable homes and can be made of cloth, leather or other materials, with wooden poles as supports. Harsh climate and hostile landscapes force nomadic communities to move with the seasons to find fertile pastures for their animals and themselves. In some nomadic groups, entire families of parents, children and grandparents move together with their herd. They carry all their belongings, and put up their tents where they find water and grazing grounds.

Babur, founder of Mughal dynasty, seated under a tent watching a wrestling game

Tents are easy to put up and take down, and are used even today as shelters for festive celebrations like Durga Puja.

11000 BC – 7000 BC, Nomadic bands become larger and temporarily settle down in natural shelters

2500 BC   2000 BC   1500 BC   1000 BC   500 BC

Hunters, food-gatherers and pastoral communities do not live in one place, but usually make long seasonal journeys in search of food and pastures for their animals. Nomadic life has been prevalent through the centuries and there are several nomadic communities in India today.

The Bakkarwal Story

The Bakkarwals of Jammu and Kashmir take their herd of goats and sheep to green mountain-ous pastures in the summer, and come down to the warmer valleys and plains in winter. The Bakkarwals have travelled across this region for so many years that they have acquired vast knowledge of medicinal plants and other secrets of their natural environment.

Approximately 7 per cent of India's population is nomadic. What should we do to allow these communities to practice their traditional way of living?

2000 AD. Nomadic communities like the Bakkarwals of Kashmir still exist today

500 BC   0   500 AD   1000 AD   1500 AD   2000 AD

Settling Down

Growing crops and raising cattle required constant attention, and communities began to live near their farms and around major water resources. Such settlements led to the development of villages.

A settled life required more permanent homes, but some members of the community continued to live in tents or impermanent shelters, to hunt, fish, gather fruits and medicinal plants from nearby forests.

Linear Settlements

Houses are built along riverbanks, main roads leading to the market, a highway or a railway line.

16

10000 – 5000 BC, Domestication of plants and animals; elaborate agricultural tools; houses of mud-brick and stone

7000 BC, Mehrgarh (Pakistan), one of the earliest agricultural settlements

2500 BC	2000 BC	1500 BC	1000 BC	500 BC

By observing the annual cycle of nature, the blossoming of flowers followed by the ripening of fruits, human communities innovated a variety of agricultural practices and skills. Between 10000 and 5000 BC, people created more efficient stone tools to make it easier to grow their own food. They began to understand how irrigation, climate and seasons influenced the growth of crops.

Settlement Patterns
Villages of various types developed near water sources, raw materials and other resources. Each village had its own name, homes and farms, markets or weekly haats, places for worship and education, common lands for grazing cattle and open grounds to celebrate fairs and festivals.

Isolated Settlements
Houses are set apart depending on the size of their farms.

Even today, more than 70% of India's population continues to live in rural areas.

Nucleated Settlements
Houses are built close together around a common focus or resources — a lake, a fort, a market, a village centre or a religious building. Such villages often developed into towns.

7 Making a Home

A traditional house in Gujarat

thatch

mud

The round shape reduces the surface area exposed to the sun, cold winds and sandstorms.

TRADITIONAL HOMES

Livestock such as sheep and yaks are kept in the lower floor of the house which helps to warm the living area.

A mountain house in Kashmir

wood

A haveli in Rajasthan

stone

In the extreme desert climate, stone keeps the house cool in summer and warm in winter.

These bungalows were protected from the hot afternoon sun and rain by large verandahs that also allowed in cool breezes.

A bungalow from the British period

tile

brick

A traditional Kerala home

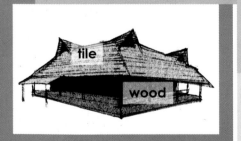

tile

wood

Kerala has two monsoons in a year. The roofs of these houses slope to allow rain water to drain off.

The entire house rests on wooden stilts to keep it safely away from flooding water.

A house in Meghalaya

thatch

wood

18

6000-600 BC, Houses built on stone foundations; clusters of circular houses with common courtyard begin to appear

2500 BC, Harappan houses of baked bricks

| 2500 BC | 2000 BC | 1500 BC | 1000 BC | 500 BC |

India has distinct geographical zones where human beings have lived for hundreds of years and created their own unique culture. For example, desert communities have a different way of life to those who live by the sea, or from people who live in the mountains.

Unique Designs
While houses in a village are similar in shape and style, each home is unique in the way it is decorated by the women of the house.

Old ways of building homes are under threat. Sometimes unsuitable modern building techniques and materials are preferred to traditional, eco-friendly skills and practices.

Courtyard of a house in the Rajasthan desert painted with geometric patterns

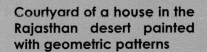

Decorated door in Orchha, a village in Madhya Pradesh

Decorated entrance to a house in Rajasthan

A Kolam pattern from Tamil Nadu

Lime powder, a natural disinfectant, prevents insects and termites from infesting the house. Using lime powder, homes are re-plastered and decorated after the monsoon, in preparation for weddings, festivals and other celebrations.

19

Villages

Villages along riverbanks grew rich and produced enough surplus food beyond the immediate needs of the community, making it possible for some people to have more free time. Time away from agriculture gave people the opportunity to learn specialized skills such as crafts and the business of trade. New skills led to the strengthening of village economies, and some of them expanded into large towns and cities.

Towns and Cities

A town is where the primary occupation is not farming, but its residents are employed in a range of activities — trading, education, the arts, administration and governance.

Ghats at Varanasi on the Ganga, U.P.

Civilizations

A civilization denotes the expansion of cities, population and the emergence of urban city life.

- 3000 BC, Earliest evidence of writing in Mesopotamia
- 3000 BC, Increase in size of villages
- 2780 BC, First pyramid designed in Egypt
- 2500-1500 BC, Harappan Civilization
- 2300 BC, Trade between the Harappans and the Mesopotamian culture
- c.1000-600 BC, Craftsmen become specialized

2500 BC   2000 BC   1500 BC   1000 BC   500 BC

Many ancient civilizations grew along the banks of major rivers. Rivers that flow from the mountains to the plains bring soil rich in minerals that is good for agriculture. Self-sufficient village economies where the primary occupation is farming led to the concentration of settlements that evolved into towns and cities.

BLACK SEA

Yellow River

TERRANEAN SEA

IRAQ

Euphrates

Tigris

CHINA

EGYPT

PAKISTAN

Indus   Ghaggar-Hakra

INDIA

PACIFIC OCEAN

Nile

ARABIAN SEA

BAY OF BENGAL

INDIAN OCEAN

Transportation   Paper

Animals   Defence

Plants   Medicine

Fish   RIVERS   Food

Recreation   Sanitation

Irrigation

Drinking   Bathing

Bricks   Washing

Dishes   WATER   Clothes

To put out fires

CIVILIZATIONS OF THE ANCIENT WORLD

Mesopotamian Civilization between the Rivers Tigris and Euphrates Valley (now Iraq)

Egyptian Civilization along the River Nile

Harappan Civilization along the Rivers Indus and Ghaggar-Hakra (now India and Pakistan)

Chinese Civilization along the Yellow River

Over the last 50 years, the Ganga has become highly polluted. One of the largest concentrations of people on earth is found along its banks. Chemicals from industry, sewage and human as well as livestock waste are among the causes of pollution of this great river.

21

c. 0-300 AD, Specialized craft centers emerge across the country

500 BC   0   500 AD   1000 AD   1500 AD   2000 AD

9   The Harappan Civilization

City Plan

These 5,000-year-old cities were well planned:

Main roads were intersected by side lanes

Workshop areas were provided for craft production

Large mud-brick platforms were used for large structures

Granaries or warehouses were built

Residential areas were to the east of the city

Well-drained bathrooms were linked to the town's covered drainage system

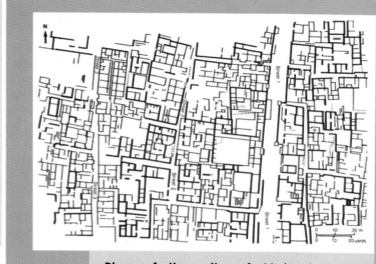

Plan of the city of Mohenjodaro, present day Pakistan

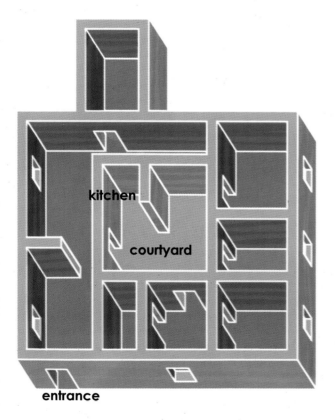

kitchen

courtyard

entrance

Harappan house

A typical Harappan house had the following features:

A flat roof

Some were two storeyed

Houses were built of baked bricks of standard size

Doors opened on to the street

Living areas were built around a courtyard

Each house had a kitchen and a well for water

> ! The National Museum in New Delhi has the world's largest collection of objects from the Harappan Civilization.

2500-1500 BC, Harappan Civilization

1700 BC, Decline of Harappan Civilization — 1500 BC, First wave of Aryan Invasion

2500 BC   2000 BC   1500 BC   1000 BC   500 BC

The 1920's discovery of Mohenjodaro confirmed that India, like Egypt and China, was home to one of the oldest civilizations of the world. Over 1,000 cities have been excavated covering an area of 1,000 sq km around the Indus and the Ghaggar-Hakra rivers, in Pakistan and northwestern India, making it the most extensive civilization of its time.

City Economy

Harappan cities were centres of trade and commerce. The economy was supported by food grown in villages that was transported to towns and cities by bullock cart or boat. Traders also established trade links with Southern India, Afghanistan, Mesopotamia and Iran.

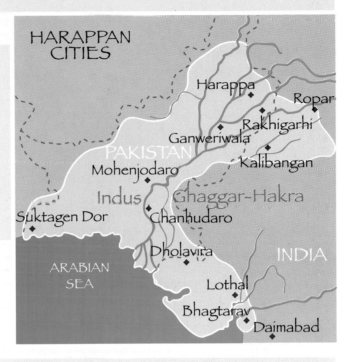

HARAPPAN CITIES

Harappa
Ropar
Rakhigarhi
Ganweriwala
PAKISTAN
Kalibangan
Mohenjodaro
Indus   Ghaggar-Hakra
Suktagen Dor   Chanhudaro
Dholavira   INDIA
ARABIAN SEA
Lothal
Bhagtarav
Daimabad

Seal with horned figure surrounded by animals, National Museum, New Delhi

Seals

Carefully graded weights and measures, and seals (steatite tablets) with merchant's trading signs suggest that these cities grew prosperous through trade. Thousands of seals were found stamped on goods indicating ownership of the goods. Each seal has engraved on it an animal motif or design, and a script that has not yet been deciphered. When the script is understood, we will learn lots more about this incredibly sophisticated urban culture and its people.

Seal engraved with bull symbol and script

Ruins of the city of Mohenjodaro, Pakistan

Why these Cities Were Lost and Forgotten

Excavations suggest that there were many floods and fires, but the inhabitants kept rebuilding these cities after each disaster. There may have been an earthquake that changed the course of the river and forced people to desert their cities. Some of the cities survived for over 1,000 years. Around 1700 BC, people gradually moved to safer, more fertile places.

23

500 BC   0   500 AD   1000 AD   1500 AD   2000 AD

10 The Harappan Arts & After

Metal Sculpture
This period is called the Bronze Age. From the 5,000-year-old 'Dancing Girl', we know that the people of this civilization knew how to mine metal, transport it, make bronze (an alloy) and cast it to make sculptures.

Bronze statue of Dancing Girl, Mohenjodaro, Pakistan

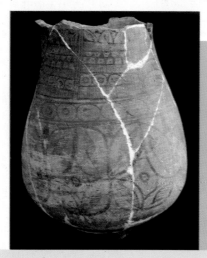

Decorated pot, Lothal, Gujarat

Pottery
Expert potters made wheel-thrown pottery. Pots of different shapes suggest that they were used for storage of water, others for food grain, for cooking and eating.

Harappan pottery is distinct with designs of plants, birds and abstract forms painted in black on a red surface.

Weaving
Discovery of weaving tools such as spindles and bobbins from Harappan sites indicate that people knew the art of spinning and weaving cloth 5,000 years ago.

Jewellery
Harappan craftsmen, like those from Mesopotamia and Egypt, were way ahead of their time. Elegantly designed bangles, necklaces and other jewellery made of gold, silver, semi-precious stones, shell and other materials have been discovered in several Harappan cities.

Clay toy, Mohenjodaro, Pakistan

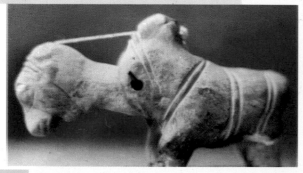

Toys
Thousands of clay toys have been found in cities of the Harappan civilization. These toys were designed especially to entertain children. Some with movable heads; little toy carts (the oldest example of a wheeled vehicle), whistles shaped like birds, a squirrel eating a nut, a lady kneading dough, a woman holding a baby are among the several toys crafted by the Harappan people.

1400-1000 BC. Advent of iron associated with Black & Red Ware and Grey Ware cultures   600-300 BC. NBP Ware

| 2500 BC | 2000 BC | 1500 BC | 1000 BC | 500 BC |

As Harappan cities grew, they supported more people with different occupations. From the objects found in these cities, we know that the people were skilled in a variety of crafts such as pottery, weaving, metalwork, toy, bead and brick making. They were also aware of the principles of engineering and mathematics.

Pots Tell it All

The discovery of 2,000-year-old pottery across India suggests that farming communities continued to live in villages even after the Harappan civilization. Some of these communities have been named after their pottery — the Black on Red Ware culture (c.1400-1000 BC); the Painted Grey Ware culture (c.1100-350 BC) and the Northern Black Polished Ware culture (c. 600-300 BC).

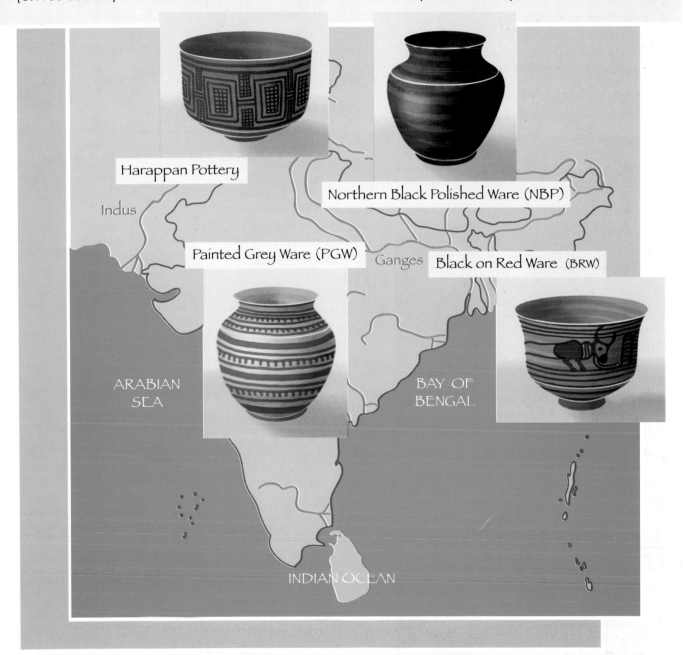

Harappan Pottery

Northern Black Polished Ware (NBP)

Indus

Painted Grey Ware (PGW)   Ganges   Black on Red Ware (BRW)

ARABIAN SEA

BAY OF BENGAL

INDIAN OCEAN

Pottery once fired, is so long lasting that it leaves its trail even after 4,000 years!

500 BC   0   500 AD   1000 AD   1500 AD   2000 AD

Literary Arts

India has two major literary traditions.

Oral Tradition: Stories, poems, riddles, rhymes that are spoken and memorized but have never been written down. That is why oral traditions are very difficult to preserve.

Written Tradition: India has 18 national languages and about 1,652 dialects and regional languages. Each language and dialect has its own history of poetry, novels and stories, plays and drama.

Priests chanting hymns

Story Telling

Human beings have always loved to tell stories, and also listen to tales from far away lands. It is through the medium of story telling, folk tales, puppetry, songs, poetry and rhymes that early communities preserved knowledge and passed it on to the next generation. The Vedas — our most ancient texts — were composed as hymns and written down only after several hundred years.

Scroll painting, Rajasthan

Bhopas of Rajasthan and Patuas of West Bengal travel from village to village narrating stories using painted pictures, songs and poetry.

Rig Veda

The Rig Veda has 1,028 verses that describe the life of pastoral communities. These groups moved across the north-western regions to live in the area of the Sapta Sindhava or seven rivers and tributaries of the Indus.

Sama Veda

The Sama Veda is the Book of Music. This is our earliest record of music and tells us how the Rig Veda was chanted.

Yajur Veda

The Yajur Veda is the Book of Sacrifice. It describes several rites and rituals in detail: how they must be performed and the verses that accompany the ceremony.

Atharva Veda

The Atharva Veda is the book of magic and spells. It has special chants to cure diseases and ailments.

Upanishadas and Puranas

Upanishadas and Puranas are the source of India's philosophy and mythology.

850 BC, First known composition of the Mahabharat

1000-600 BC, The three later Vedas are composed

1500 BC, Rig Veda, earliest literary text composed

2500 BC   2000 BC   1500 BC   1000 BC   500 BC

New settlements grew in different parts of the subcontinent, along the Ganges, the Indus and other rivers such as the Krishna, Godavari, Pennar and Kaveri. The discovery of iron — a new metal, led to the making of even more efficient tools for farming, allowing people to have more free time for creative expression that gave birth to a whole range of literature.

Mahabharata

The Mahabharata has 100,000 verses and it is the second longest epic poem in the world. The epic is a collection of tales with several stories and sub-stories. The Pandavas (five brothers) and their common wife Draupadi are defeated in a game of dice, and lose their kingdom to their cousins, the hundred Kaurava brothers. They are forced into exile, where many events take place. The Pandavas then return to fight a great battle (the Mahabharata) against the Kauravas to regain their kingdom.

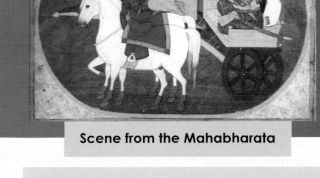

Scene from the Mahabharata

Kathakali puppet of Bhim, Kerala

Ramayana

The Ramayana, another great ancient Indian epic in Sanskrit, is said to have been composed by the legendary saint Valmiki. The epic has over 100,000 lines that tell the story of a young prince, Rama, his wife Sita and brother Lakshmana, and the years they spent in exile. While they lived in the forest, Ravana, the king of Lanka, kidnapped Sita. After a fierce battle, Rama and his army rescue Sita and return triumphant to their kingdom. The defeat of Ravana is celebrated as Dussehra, while the festival of Diwali marks Rama's jubilant homecoming.

The Ramayana is a popular story all over India. It is told through dance, theatre, puppet shows, comic books and television. There are many versions of the story as it travelled to foreign lands like Thailand, Cambodia and Java, there too it influenced the building of temples, dance forms and the art of puppetry.

Sculptural panel depicting the Ramayana, Kailash Temple, Ellora, Maharashtra

Puppet of Ravana, West Bengal

100 BC-100 AD, The Bhagvada Gita is composed

500 BC — 0 — 500 AD — 1000 AD — 1500 AD — 2000 AD

12 Story of the Buddha

Look at the picture of the Sarnath sculpture and follow the story of the Buddha.

1
The ruler of the Sakas had a beautiful wife called Mahamaya, who one night had an auspicious dream of a white elephant. Astrologers had predicted that Mahamaya would have a son who would be a gift to mankind: a great sage or a great king.

2
Mahamaya stopped on her way to her mother's house at the gardens of Lumbini (Nepal) and gave birth to a baby boy, called Siddharth.

3
Siddharth grew up in the palace at Kapilavastu (Nepal). One day he saw an old man, a sick man, a dead man being taken for cremation, and a sage or sadhu. He wondered why life had to be so sad and what could make people happy.

7
The Buddha's disciples persuaded him to go to Sarnath (Uttar Pradesh). At the Deer Park, he gave his first public teaching. He also set up the Sangha or Buddhist order for monks.

6
Siddharth meditated for 40 days and nights and attained nirvana or Budh (wisdom). From that time on he was called the Buddha, the Peepal tree where he meditated was called the Bodhi tree and Gaya came to be called Bodh Gaya (Bihar).

5
He shaved off his hair, wore simple clothes and travelled far and wide meeting gurus and holy men and discussing the meaning of life.

4
Soon after this disturbing incident, Siddharth decided to leave his palace, riding his horse, Kanthaka.

Around the age of 80, the Buddha passed away in Kushinagara.

28

566-486 BC, Age of the Buddha

2500 BC   2000 BC   1500 BC   1000 BC   500 BC

One of India's greatest teachers lived 2,500 years ago. Born into a royal family, Siddharth Gautam gave up his life of luxury and attained nirvana to become the Buddha, or the enlightened one. Stories of the Buddha in his various incarnations are called 'Jataka Kathas'.

MAHAKAPI JATAKA

Look at the Mahakapi sculpture from the Stupa at Bharut (Madhya Pradesh) now in the Indian Museum in Kolkata. The sculpture tells a story from the Jataka in which the Buddha is a kind and compassionate teacher.

1. The great Monkey King and his tribe of 80,000 lived near the river Ganga.

2. One day the King of Varanasi went to capture the monkeys with his army.

3. The Monkey King realized the danger and stretched his body across the river to make a bridge so that his tribe of monkeys could escape.

4. There was one monkey who hated the Monkey King. He jumped on the King with great force to try and kill him.

5. The King of Varanasi was so touched by the Monkey King's gesture of sacrifice that he begged forgiveness and became the Buddha's faithful student.

100 AD. Jataka Tales composed

500 BC   0   500 AD   1000 AD   1500 AD   2000 AD

Harmika
The tiered umbrella that represents the steps to heaven. The umbrella is also symbolic of shade that is provided to great teachers, and also represents the Bodhi tree under which the Buddha attained nirvana.

Anda
The hemispherical shape of the mound. In Sanskrit, the word means the egg that symbolizes spiritual birth.

Sanchi Stupa No.3, Sanchi, M.P.

Vedika with Torans
The railings with grand gateways were erected around the stupa, in imitation of older wooden ones. The gateways mark the cardinal directions so that you enter and make a pradakshina or walk (once, 3, or 7 times) around the stupa, keeping your right shoulder towards the sacred structure.

Sanchi Stupa
Sanchi in Madhya Pradesh was built on a hilltop along an important trade route. Many believe that Emperor Ashoka (273-232 BC) built Sanchi Stupa No.1 in brick. The mound was later covered in stone. From the 2nd century BC, for over 1,000 years, Sanchi was a vibrant Buddhist centre with several stupas and monasteries.

Pillar Stories
The great torans of Sanchi are beautifully carved with stories from the Jatakas. As the pilgrim performed the pradakshina, they could interpret and learn the stories of the life of the Buddha.

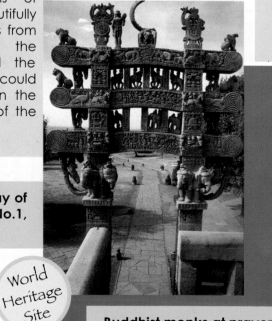

Toran or gateway of Sanchi Stupa No.1, Sanchi, M.P.

World Heritage Site

Buddhist monks at prayer

2500 BC   2000 BC   1500 BC   1000 BC   500 BC

After the Buddha died, his relics or remains of his bones were divided amongst Buddhist followers. These relics were placed in a crystal or stone casket, and buried inside a mud mound. Over time, the mud mound was made larger, covered in stone and called the stupa — an important place of Buddhist worship.

Stupas

Stupas enshrining relics of the Buddha or famous Buddhist saints were built in countries where the Buddha's teachings spread.

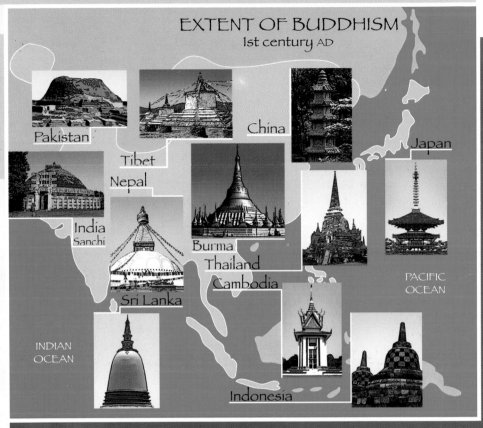

EXTENT OF BUDDHISM
1st century AD

Pakistan
China
Japan
Tibet
Nepal
India
Sanchi
Burma
Thailand
Cambodia
Sri Lanka
PACIFIC OCEAN
INDIAN OCEAN
Indonesia

Worship of the Bodhi tree, Sanchi, M.P.

Festivals

The full moon or Purnima of the month of May is celebrated as Buddha Jayanti. In Sri Lanka, every full moon is celebrated as a holiday and the Bodhi tree is decorated. Thousands of Buddhists from around the world visit places associated with the Buddha, like Bodh Gaya. Famous living monasteries in India are Hemis in Ladakh, Rumtek in Sikkim and Dharamsala in Himachal Pradesh.

Terms for the Stupa

Bhutan	**Chorten**
Burma	**Pagoda**
Cambodia	**Caitya**
India	**Stupa** (except in Ladakh where it is known as **Chorten**)
Indonesia	**Candi**
Japan	**To** (means 'tower')
Nepal	**Caitya**
Sri Lanka	**Dagoba/Chaitiya**
Thailand	**Chedi**
Tibet	**Chorten**

272-232 BC, Reign of Ashoka
240 BC, Buddhism reaches Sri Lanka
1st century AD, Buddhism spreads to Thailand, Burma, China

| 500 BC | 0 | 500 AD | 1000 AD | 1500 AD | 2000 AD |

14   Image of the Buddha

Buddha Across the World

As Buddhism travelled across the world (from India to Afghanistan, Nepal, Tibet, Sri Lanka, Thailand, Cambodia, China and Japan), we can see how the face of the Buddha changes in each region.

Buddha image, Sarnath, U.P., India

Buddha image, Mathura, U.P., India

Buddha image, Japan

Buddha image, Sri Lanka

Buddha image, Burma

Hinayana

In this period the presence of the Buddha is represented by symbols, like the Bodhi tree, the wheel of law, the stupa, his footprints and the empty throne.

Mahayana

In this tradition of Buddhism, images of the Buddha were the centre of worship in the prayer hall.

32

| 2500 BC | 2000 BC | 1500 BC | 1000 BC | 500 BC |

Kings, noblemen, visitors from foreign lands and ordinary people were all attracted to the Buddha's great wisdom. His teachings are still widely accepted the world over.

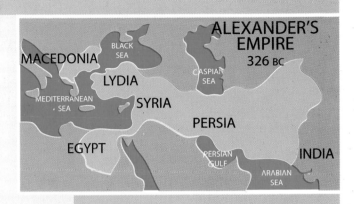

ALEXANDER'S EMPIRE

326 BC

MACEDONIA
BLACK SEA
LYDIA
MEDITERRANEAN SEA
CASPIAN SEA
SYRIA
PERSIA
EGYPT
PERSIAN GULF
ARABIAN SEA
INDIA

The Buddha's Eightfold Path

1. Right Understanding
2. Right Thought
3. Right Speech
4. Right Action
5. Right Livelihood
6. Right Effort
7. Right Mindfulness
8. Right Concentration

Alexander the Great

Buddha image, Tibet

Buddha image, Gandhara region, present day Pakistan and Afghanistan

Alexander the Great

Alexander was nineteen years old when he became king and always dreamed of being ruler of the whole world. In his days, the most powerful kingdom was Persia. Alexander travelled with his army from Macedonia in Greece, and defeated the Persians in 331 BC.

Alexander then heard of the greatness and wealth of India and entered the north-western region in 326 BC defeating Porus, another brave king. Soon his army became homesick and they began their journey homeward. Alexander died on the way home.

Even though Alexander died at the young age of 32 years, he brought India in touch with Greece over 2,000 years ago. This led to an exchange of ideas as administrators and merchants from Greece settled in a region called Gandhara (parts of Afghanistan and Pakistan) and met artists and thinkers from India. Local artistic traditions and styles were influenced by these Grecian visitors.

327-325 BC, Alexander's invasion
190 BC, Greek settlements in North-West
320 AD, Rise of Gupta dynasty
552 AD, Buddhism reaches Japan
641 AD, Buddhism reaches Tibet

500 BC   0   500 AD   1000 AD   1500 AD   2000 AD

15 In the Footsteps of Mahavir

Life of Mahavir
Mahavir Jain was born to a princely family, and like the Buddha, he also left his home and material belongings to become a teacher of ahimsa. In sculptures, he is depicted as standing or seated in deep meditation.

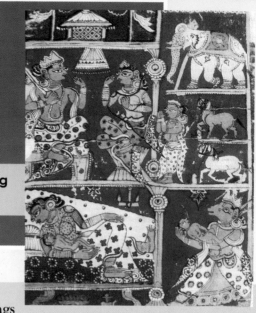

Jain painting depicting the birth of Mahavir

Teachings
Mahavir taught the message of peace in which he explained that ahimsa or non-injury to all is the path that will free us from the endless cycle of birth and death.

Tribute to the Tirthankara
Shravanabelagola, in Karnataka, has a huge statue made out of a single block of stone 17.7 metres high. This statue is one of the largest in the world and represents Bahubali, son of the first Tirthankara. It is said that Bahubali left his kingdom and stood in meditation without moving for a whole year. The sculpture shows how creepers and plants grew beside and around this gentle calm saint.

Statue of Bahubali Gomateshwara, Shravanabelagola, Karnataka

Festivals
Mahavir Jayanthi is celebrated every year in India on the birthday of Mahavir.

Every twelve years, a special celebration is organized at Shravanabelagola and the giant figure of Bahubali is bathed with bucketfuls of milk and honey.

Helping the Helpless
Jainism teaches ahimsa or non-injury to others. The Jain tirthankaras teach us not to harm human beings, animals, birds and even insects. Delhi has a famous bird hospital set up by the Jain community, where an injured bird can be brought for treatment and recovery.

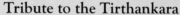

c. 540 BC, Birth of Mahavir

2500 BC   2000 BC   1500 BC   1000 BC   500 BC

There are 24 Jain tirthankaras or great teachers, all of whom show us by their own example how to lead a good life without hurting anyone or anything. Mahavir was one such saintly person.

The Jain Mandir

The Jain temple is similar to a Hindu temple. Each region and state in India has evolved its own style. The garbha griha has a tirthankara (the main image) in a standing or seated position. There is a hall or mandap in the front of the temple where devotees worship. The outer wall of the temple is carved with bands of sculptures with images of the tirthankars.

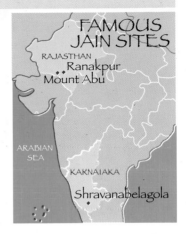

FAMOUS JAIN SITES

RAJASTHAN
Ranakpur
Mount Abu

ARABIAN SEA

KARNATAKA

Shravanabelagola

Jain temple complex, Rajasthan

Mount Abu, Rajasthan

When major temples of Khajuraho, Bhubaneshwar and Thanjavur were being built in the 10th century, the Solanki Kings and rich Jain merchants of Gujarat built a group of magnificent Jain shrines on a hill top, Mount Abu. The Dilvara Temple is the most famous of these shrines. From the outside the temple looks plain, but from the inside every inch of marble is richly carved with sculptured panels of dancers, musicians, horses and elephants. The marble for the temples of Mount Abu were brought from several miles away, and carried up the steep hill to create a calm white atmosphere of the Jain mandir.

Carved marble ceiling of a Jain temple, Ranakpur, Rajasthan

Marble interior of a Jain temple

Carved pillar of a Jain temple, Mount Abu, Rajasthan

10th Century AD, Image of Gomateshwara, Shravanabelagola ⌐ ⌐ c. 1032 AD, The first Dilvara temple, Mt. Abu

| 500 BC | 0 | 500 AD | 1000 AD | 1500 AD | 2000 AD |

What is a Kingdom?

Political authority — with a king, military and administrative systems

Concentration of many different types of people

Several types of natural resources

Urban centres where crafts developed

Villages that produced food

The Mauryan Kingdom

Chandragupta Maurya came from an ordinary family. He once heard a mother scolding her child, "Don't eat food from the centre of the plate, where the food will be hot and you will burn your tongue. Eat from the side of the plate, where the food is a little cooler." Using this advice to guide him, Chandragupta decided to capture Pataliputra (present day Patna), a famous town in those days, by first conquering the less protected (cooler) villages and towns around it. Chandragupta Maurya then formed a large empire and made Pataliputra his capital.

Chandragupta, helped by his clever friend and minister Chanakya (author of the Arthashashtra), developed ways to govern a kingdom well, with rules on how to pay taxes, how to run a good administrative system, an army, and how to keep the citizens safe and happy.

Emperor Ashoka

Ashoka, Chandragupta's grandson used an inge-nious method to communicate rules and regula-tions of his government to the people. Throughout his kingdom, simple messages in Pali (a less difficult form of Sanskrit using the Brahmi script) were carved on pillars and rocks.

Ashokan inscription in the Brahmi script

Translation of a Minor Edict of Ashoka
"Obey mother and father, obey the teach-ers, have mercy on living beings, spread the truth. These virtues of Dhamma should be followed."

$+$ = ka   þ = da   φ = va

$\curlyvee$ = ma   ↓ = ya   ⊥ = na

The inscriptions of Ashoka are in the Brahmi script that is the ancestor of most Indian scripts.

600 BC, Towns develop in North India; Beginning of coinage

2500 BC   2000 BC   1500 BC   1000 BC   500 BC

Over the centuries, settlements along fertile river valleys grew into the grama (village) and towns (with name endings like 'pura' — Hastinapura). By 600 BC, around the time of the Buddha and Mahavir, kingdoms were divided into territories called janapadas, and mahajanapadas.

Terracotta sculpture, Bihar

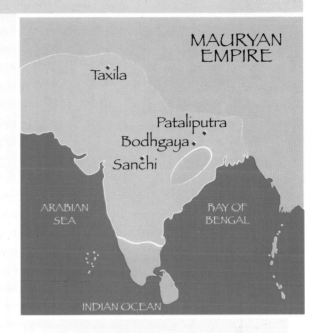

MAURYAN EMPIRE

Taxila

Pataliputra
Bodhgaya
Sanchi

ARABIAN SEA

BAY OF BENGAL

INDIAN OCEAN

Indian national flag

Mauryan coins

Lion Capital of Sarnath

Sacred Buddhist symbols and images were carved on great sandstone pillars to mark famous sites. After independence in 1947, the Lion Capital of Sarnath made during the time of Ashoka in the 3rd century BC, was chosen as the symbol of the Indian Republic. The capital is adorned with four lions protecting the four directions — north, south, east and west. On the lower border, it has four dharmachakras or wheels of dharma or duty. Separating the wheels is a bull (devotion), an elephant (strength), a lion (power) and a horse (speed).

Lion Capital, Mauryan dynasty, Sarnath, U.P.

321-185 BC, Mauryan Empire

500 BC   0   500 AD   1000 AD   1500 AD   2000 AD

In the 2nd century BC, an extraordinary innovation in architecture took place. Buildings were cut into, and out of solid rock. First the door was cut out of the rock face, then the hall and rooms were cut inside the hill. The hard black volcanic rock of the Western Ghats was most suitable for rock-cut architecture and the kind of difficult carving seen at Ajanta.

Ajanta is a World Heritage Site for three reasons: its Buddhist rock-cut architecture, its sculpture and its mural paintings.

From Wood to Stone

In the Chaitya Hall at Ajanta, there is a large image of the Buddha seated in front of the sculptured stupa.

The hall has all the features of a wooden building such as beams on the roof. In rock-cut architecture, however, beams serve no purpose because they are not carrying the weight of the building. These features give us an idea of how wooden structures were made and what these older buildings looked like, as none of them exist today.

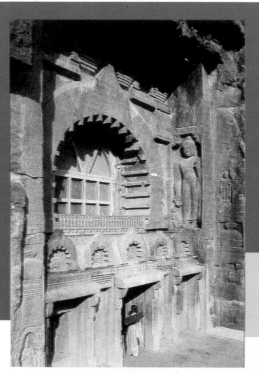

Façade of Chaitya Griha, Ajanta Caves, Maharashtra

Chaitya Griha with seated Buddha, Ajanta Caves, Maharashtra

Conjectural reconstruction of wooden building

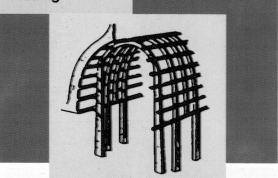

2500 BC   2000 BC   1500 BC   1000 BC   500 BC

In February 1824, an English army officer, James Alexander, was out hunting in the Western Ghats when he heard from the local people about the Ajanta Caves near Aurangabad. It was he who told the western world about the wonders that he saw there.

Exterior view of Ajanta caves, Maharashtra

World Heritage Site

Ajanta's Horseshoe Shape

Work started here in the 2nd century BC and continued for 800 years along a horseshoe shaped natural cliff looking over the river Waghora. Several chaityas (prayer halls with a stupa within) and viharas (dormitories) were carved out of the hill for the monks to live and pray in a peaceful and quiet environment.

Ajanta Paintings

The paintings of Ajanta are world famous. They have been painted with natural colours provided by the volcanic rock of the Deccan plateau: black from crushed coal, white from lime, ochre and red from natural rocks and minerals. These paints were applied to the dry plaster layer on the rock surface.

Bodhisattva, Cave No. 1, Ajanta Caves, Maharashtra

The Buddha before his wife Yashodhara and son Rahul, Cave No. 17, Ajanta Caves, Maharashtra

Unfortunately, the humid human breath of visitors is causing the plaster of the paintings to peel off the walls. Do you think the number of visitors to Ajanta should be restricted?

2nd Century BC–5th Century AD, Ajanta Caves, near Aurangabad

| 500 BC | 0 | 500 AD | 1000 AD | 1500 AD | 2000 AD |

Jewish Communities of India

Judaism is practiced in India by several Jewish communities who came to the country from the region of West Asia several hundred years ago. Some of these are:

The Bene Israel Jews

The Cochin Jews

The Baghdadi Jews

The Bnei Menashe Jews who live in Mizoram

💀

Unfortunately, today there are less than 17,000 Jewish people in India. Most of the community has left for Israel and other parts of the world.

Hebrew Bible

The most important book for the Jewish people is the Torah in the Hebrew language. The Torah describes how God created the universe and all its creatures. It also tells the story of great prophets who showed people the way to live peaceful and honest lives.

Moses

Moses was a prophet of the Jewish people. The Pharaohs of ancient Egypt were very cruel. One of them ordered the killing of all the male children of the Jewish people living in Egypt. One family put their child in a basket and floated it down the river. The Pharaohs's daughter found it, and kept the baby, who grew up to be the wise Moses. Moses freed the Jewish people and led them out of Egypt back into Israel. The first five books of the Hebrew Bible are called the 'Five Books of Moses' or the Torah.

Special Days

Sabbath or Saturday is the day of rest, when no work is done.

Rosh Hashannah is the New Year or the celebration of creation, or the world's birthday!

Moses with the 10 commandments

Teachings

It was at Mount Sinai (Egypt), where Moses received the Torah (law) from God in the form of the 10 commandments:

1. I am the Lord
2. You should not worship images
3. Do not take god's name in vain
4. Observe the day of Sabbath
5. Respect your mother and father
6. Do not murder
7. Do not commit adultery
8. Do not steal
9. Do not be a false witness
10. Do not feel envy

| 2500 BC | 2000 BC | 1500 BC | 1000 BC | 500 BC |

The earliest known Jewish settlers in India came to the country to trade in spices such as pepper. A small group settled in Kerala in the first century AD.

Keneseth Eliyahoo Synagogue, Mumbai, Maharashtra

JEWISH TRADERS COME TO INDIA
1st century AD

SYRIA
ISRAEL
JORDAN
IRAQ
IRAN
PERSIAN GULF
INDIA
Mumbai
ARABIAN SEA
Cochin
INDIAN OCEAN

everlasting lamp

bimah

blue tiles

Synagogue interior, Cochin, Kerala

The Synagogue

Followers of the Jewish faith worship in a 'Synagogue', which means meeting place. Jewish people built Synagogues wherever they travelled for trade.

The Synagogue in Cochin, Kerala, is the oldest surviving synagogue in the country. Built in 1568 and renovated many times, it is situated along a cobbled street similar to those in the olden days in Jerusalem. The **Everlasting Lamp** in the Synagogue symbolizes a constant sacred presence. The Torah is capped by two golden crowns given by the Maharaja of Travancore and Cochin, who generously gave the Jewish trading community the right to live and trade in Kerala. The floor is paved with 19th-century **white and blue tiles** from China, also part of the sea trade route from Asia to Europe. There is a raised platform or **bimah** for the person leading the prayers. The congregation (people who gather to pray) face the direction of their most holy city, Jerusalem in Israel.

The ritual of Bar (Boy) and Bat (Girl) Mitzvah

When Jewish boys and girls reach the age of 13, a special function called Bar or Bat Mitzvah is held. During this occasion children are initiated into the Jewish faith, and are formally accepted into the community.

> Pepper was called 'black gold' as it was much in demand in Europe. In the days when there were no refrigerators and meat got very smelly, pepper, the magic spice, was used to improve the taste.

1st Century AD, Arrival of Jewish settlers; Internal and external trade thrives
c.1 AD, Arab sailors discover monsoon winds while crossing the Arabian Sea to India

500 BC   0   500 AD   1000 AD   1500 AD   2000 AD

Life of Christ

Jesus Christ lived 2,000 years ago in Judea (Israel) which was ruled by foreign Roman invaders. He was born in Bethlehem (also in Israel), and his birthday is celebrated as Christmas on the 25th of December each year. Jesus was brought up by Mary, his mother, and Joseph his father, who was a carpenter.

When Jesus was a young man he began to perform many wonderful miracles like feeding thousands of pilgrims with just two loaves of bread, and curing sick people. He had many followers who believed he was the Son of God, and his popularity made other Jewish people and the Roman rulers angry. He had twelve close friends called the disciples. However, one of the disciples betrayed him, and this led to King Herod (leader of the Jews) ordering the death of Jesus.

Jesus was nailed to a wooden cross in the same way that thieves and murderers were punished at that time. Jesus Christ is believed to have died on the cross, and was buried on Good Friday, but on the third day he rose again and appeared before his people. This day is called Easter, a festival of great celebration.

Jesus sent his disciples across the world to spread his message of love. Within 100 years after the death of Jesus (counted as 1 AD), his teachings had spread to North Africa and India.

The Bible

The Christian Holy Bible has two parts: the first is the Old Testament (same as the Hebrew Bible), followed by the New Testament that contains stories of Jesus' life and that of his disciples. Early Bibles were beautifully illustrated and written completely by hand.

2500 BC   2000 BC   1500 BC   1000 BC   500 BC

Like Jewish traders, Christian merchants came to India in the 1st century AD. It is said that Saint Thomas, a disciple of Jesus, went to South India from Syria to spread the teachings of Christ. India has a small (2.7%) percentage of Christians many of whom have significantly contributed to India's development by building schools, colleges, hospitals and charitable institutions. Mother Teresa received the Nobel Peace Prize in 1979.

The Church
The church is a place where Christians meet to pray together, and like the Mosque and the Synagogue, space is provided in the Church for congregational worship.

Bells of a church are rung to call everyone to prayer.

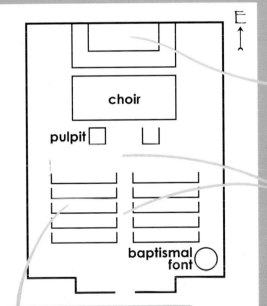

An **altar** is located at one end of the church. It is the table where the image of the cross is placed. The cross reminds everyone that Jesus gave up his life to save our lives. Objects for ceremonial worship are placed on the altar.

The **nave** is the central part of the interior of a church. The **aisles** are the spaces between the benches.

Benches are provided for people to sit on. Everyone in the church sits, stands, sings or prays according to the instructions given by the priest.

Holy Blessing
There are many types of services in a church. A baptism service is when a newborn baby is blessed by the priest with holy water. Marriages and funerals are also held in the church.

43

c. 6-4 BC – c. 30 AD,
Life of Christ
c. 50 AD, St. Thomas arrives

| 500 BC | 0 | 500 AD | 1000 AD | 1500 AD | 2000 AD |

20 Making India their Home

Prophet Zaratushtra

Religious Text
The Holy Book of the Parsis is the Zenda Avesta.

What they Believe
Since fire, one of the five elements of the Earth, purifies everything as it burns, it is considered sacred by the Parsis. Therefore, the Parsis do not burn their dead because they believe that would contaminate the sacred fire. Instead, in the Tower of Silence, they expose the dead body to the natural elements to dispose of it in a pure and organic way.

The sacred fire

Sacred Symbols
Fire is pure and cannot be polluted; hence the symbol of fire and the winged sun-disc are seen carved on all fire temples.

The sun disc

Festivals
Parsis celebrate six Ghambhar festivals that are thanksgiving ceremonies to honour the seasons and praise the creation of the world.

Nav Roz, or the first day of the New Year starts in the spring season. Homes are cleaned, and new clothes are bought for the whole family. Most families go to the Fire Temple to offer thanks for the past year, and to pray for the year to come.

2500 BC   2000 BC   1500 BC   1000 BC   500 BC

To escape religious persecution, the Parsis emigrated to India from Persia in the 8th century. They are the followers of Zoroastrianism, the ancient Persian religion founded by the prophet Zarathustra. The Parsis worship Ahura Mazda, the god of fire and light.

J.R.D. Tata

Welcomed Guests

When the Parsis first arrived in Gujarat in the 8th century, they asked the king for land but he was reluctant to give it to them for fear it would anger his own people. The Parsi priest then asked for a bowl of milk and mixed a spoon of sugar in it. With this gesture, the priest suggested that as sugar dissolves into milk — so will the Parsis live in harmony with the local community, speak the local Gujarati language, adopt the dress, and do their best to bring to their new home the fruits of their labour. The Parsis kept their promise. Several members of the community fought for India's independence from the British. Great Parsis like J.R.D. Tata, Homi Bhaba and others made significant contributions to Indian industry, science and the arts.

! When the Mughal Emperor Akbar ruled Gujarat, he kept the sacred fire burning in his court day and night, according to the custom of the Persian Kings.

☠ There are only 65,000 Parsis in India today. By 2021, there will only be 21,000. Their numbers have been dropping drastically.

Fire Temples

Parsis worship in an Agiyari or Fire Temple where fire is the centre of worship. The sacred fire is kept burning all the time and must never be allowed to extinguish. The fire temple is usually a rectangular building of simple design with no images or sculptures. People pray in the inner hall where sacred ceremonies and rituals are also performed. The Zoti, or head priest, is the only one allowed to perform ceremonies involving fire. No non-Zoroastrians are allowed to enter a fire temple.

Entrance to a fire temple, Mumbai, Maharashtra

45

8th Century AD, Parsis arrive from Persia

1640 AD, Dorabji Patel, first Parsi to reach Mumbai

500 BC — 0 — 500 AD — 1000 AD — 1500 AD — 2000 AD

Parts of a temple

The **shikhara** or roof of the temple was built directly above the garbha griha like a crown towering above.

The **garbha griha** is where the main deity or murti is kept. It is the sanctum sanctorum or the womb of the temple.

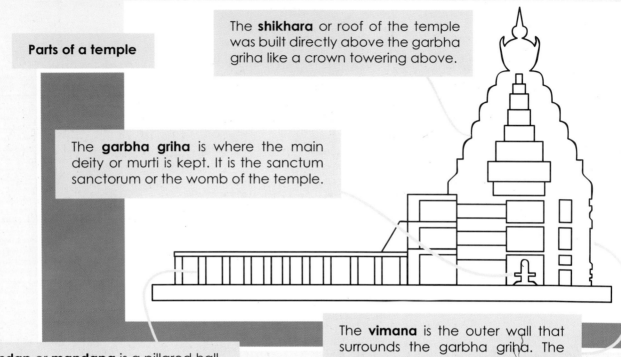

Mandap or **mandapa** is a pillared hall.

The **vimana** is the outer wall that surrounds the garbha griha. The vimana is covered with sculptures and decorative patterns, so that the pilgrim performing the pradakshina or circumambulation around the temple could easily understand the sculptured stories from the puranas, legends and myths.

Each region of India developed its own style of shikhara

The shikhara in South India is pyramidal in its outline

In Central India, the shikhara is conical in shape

In Eastern India (Orissa), the shikhara is column-like

In the Deccan region (Karnataka), the shikhara is star-shaped in plan

South India

Central India

2500 BC   2000 BC   1500 BC   1000 BC   500 BC

Devalaya means — where the gods live. The Vastushastra, the book of rules for the architect and artist, says that a temple should be built in a place 'where the gods would like to visit', with beautiful surroundings beside a river or on a hill. The name of the mandir came from the main deity, such as Hanuman mandir or Vishvanath mandir.

Draupadi and Arjun Rathas or temples, Mamallapuram, Tamil Nadu

The Beginning

The story of temple building begins at Mamallapuram on the coast of Tamil Nadu, where the Pallava kings first experimented with rock-cut carving in the 7th century. In the Mamallapuram experiment, we find the little Draupadi Mandap has a roof like a thatched village hut all carved out of one huge boulder. The builders then created the Arjuna Rath with a shikhara made up of miniature Draupadi Rath hut-like roofs in a line on all three levels. Each level of the shikhara was smaller than the last one, and this formed a pyramid-like shape characteristic of later south Indian shikharas.

World Heritage Site

Shore Temple, Mamallapuram, Tamil Nadu

The Deccan

Eastern India

Let There Be Light

Lighting the lamp is an important part of all worship. Light removes darkness just as wisdom removes ignorance. Puja or worship begins with cleaning the area, lighting of the lamp, ringing of bells, offering of fruits and flowers, burning of incense and eating of prasad, thus awakening our five senses of sight, sound, touch, smell and taste.

As we are an agricultural country, many festivals celebrate the seasons: harvesting — Pongal or Lohri during Makarsankranti (January 14th each year); beginning of summer — Holi with the splashing of colour to match the colours of the flowering trees; and beginning of the long dark nights of winter — Diwali, the festival of lights.

47

7th Century AD, Construction of rock-cut temples in South India
711 AD, Arab conquest of Sindh
600-800 AD, Distinct styles emerge in temple architecture

| 500 BC | 0 | 500 AD | 1000 AD | 1500 AD | 2000 AD |

22 Temples Cut into Rock

Exquisite Ellora

At Ellora, a small village in Maharashtra, an entire hillside was carved and cut to make 12 Buddhist Chaitya Halls and Viharas, 17 Hindu temples and 5 belonging to the Jain community. It is wonderful that so many communities of different faiths lived and created art together at this magnificent site.

World Heritage Site

Interior of Chaitya griha, Ellora Caves, Maharashtra

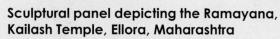

Chaitya griha, Ellora Caves, Maharashtra

Kailash Temple, Ellora Caves, Maharashtra

Sculptural panel depicting the Ramayana, Kailash Temple, Ellora, Maharashtra

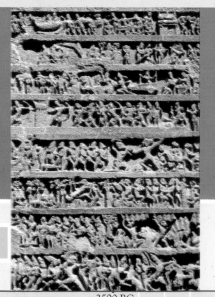

Kailash Temple

Dedicated to Lord Shiva, the famous Kailash temple has been carefully carved out of the hillside — 30 metres high, 90 metres long and 53 metres wide. This independent block of stone was cut from the top downwards to make the temple with an entrance, a hall, a high pyramid-like shikhara, elaborately carved pillars and walls.

2500 BC   2000 BC   1500 BC   1000 BC   500 BC

Artists discovered that stone was more durable than wood, and began building stone structures by copying older designs of wood and thatch buildings. Stonework was very expensive, so only important buildings were built in stone. Once confident with this new skill, artists tried all kinds of experiments with stone carving. We see early experiments in Maharashtra in Karla , Kanheri, Elephanta and Ellora.

Elephanta Island

Elephanta is the name given to an island off the coast of Mumbai by the Portuguese because they found a lovely carved stone elephant there. On this small island is a hill into which has been carved a cross-shaped hall and on each wall are larger than life sized images: Shiva and Parvati playing dice, Shiva and Parvati's wedding ceremony attended by all the gods, and the most spectacular of them all is the central image of Trimurti — Shiva with three faces, one smiling and kind, one angry and the central one peaceful.

World Heritage Site

Exterior view of Elephanta Caves, Maharashtra

Marriage of Shiva and Parvati, Elephanta Caves, Maharashtra

Trimurti of Shiva, Elephanta Caves, Maharashtra

Elephanta and Ellora in Maharashtra and Mahabalipuram in Tamil Nadu are among the best examples of rock-cut architecture. That is why these sites have been given the special World Heritage Site status, as rare places that must be protected by the entire human race.

People who live on this island do not have many facilities such as hospitals and a quick way to reach mainland Mumbai. Do you think that conservation of a heritage site must also take into consideration the people who live in its vicinity?

49

760-770 AD, Kailash temple, Ellora, near Aurangabad ⌐ ⌐ 8th-9th Century AD, Elephanta Caves, near Mumbai

| 500 BC | 0 | 500 AD | 1000 AD | 1500 AD | 2000 AD |

Kandariya Mahadev Temple, Khajuraho, M.P.

World Heritage Site

Beautiful Khajuraho

There are over 25 beautiful temples in the village of Khajuraho in Madhya Pradesh, built by the Chandella dynasty. Among the largest and most splendid is the Kandariya Mahadev temple dedicated to Lord Shiva.

Vishwanatha Temple, Khajuraho, M.P

Chandella king and queen

Shivaratri in Khajuraho

Each year, thousands of people visit Khajuraho to celebrate Mahashivaratri. They celebrate the marriage of the divine couple, Shiva and Parvati, and also enjoy a mela (fair) held especially for the event.

2500 BC   2000 BC   1500 BC   1000 BC   500 BC

The 10th-11th centuries witnessed the building of large temples abundantly decorated with sculpture and carving. Temples became centres for learning philosophy, dance and music. Thousands of pilgrims visit temple sites to participate in annual festivals and other events.

Surya Mandir

The Sun Temple built in the 13th century, on the beach in Konark, in Orissa, is designed to look like the rath or chariot, of Surya Dev, the sun god. It is believed that Surya travels round the world in a chariot driven by seven horses creating day and night. Riding on the chariot of the sun god are musicians who greet each morning with their heavenly music. To make the temple look like a chariot the artists carved 24 giant wheels and seven prancing horses made of stone. The horses are said to represent the seven days of the week or the seven colours of light.

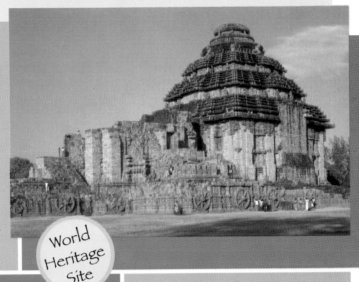

World Heritage Site

Stone wheel, Sun Temple, Konark, Orissa

The garbha griha or sanctum sanctorum of the temple has a large image of Lord Surya, a gigantic jagmohan or hall in front, and the vimana (temple wall) is covered with beautiful sculptures of musicians playing different instruments. Perhaps the tall shikara (that has now fallen) once showed sailors the way to land and safety.

Image of Surya, Sun Temple, Konark, Orissa

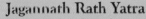

Jagannath Rath Yatra

The town of Puri comes alive in the month of July when the idol of Orissa's most revered deity, Jagannath (a form of Lord Vishnu), is taken out of the Jagannath temple in a chariot. The deity is accompanied by his sister, Subhadra, and brother, Balabhadra, in a ceremonial procession. They are then taken to Gundicha Ghar — the birthplace of Lord Jagannath, where they stay for nine days and finally return to Puri.

1017-1029 AD, Chandela rulers build the Khajuraho temple complex

1238 AD, Sun temple, Konark; Jagannath temple, Puri

| 500 BC | 0 | 500 AD | 1000 AD | 1500 AD | 2000 AD |

World Heritage Site

The Cholas of Tamil Nadu (9th–13th century)

The Chola dynasty rose to power under its king Rajaraja and then his son Rajendra Chola (1044 AD). With a good army and navy, the Cholas took territories of the Pallavas, Pandyas and Cheras. They conquered parts of Sri Lanka, the Maldives Islands and Sumatra. They then campaigned in northeastern India towards Bengal and the River Ganga. They also built several great temples in Thanjavur and Gangaikonda-cholapuram (which means the Chola city where the Ganga was brought).

Brihadeshvara Temple, Thanjavur, Tamil Nadu

Vijayanagara city complex, Hampi, Karnataka

The Chalukyas of Badami, Karnataka (6th–8th century)

The Chalukya dynasty ruled areas south of the Vindhyas in the 6th century AD. At their capital in Badami, and at Pattadakal, the kings Pulakesin I and II encouraged artists to experiment with temple designs. These designs became so popular that they later spread to different parts of India and were adopted as the regional style.

World Heritage Site

The Kings of Vijayanagara, Karnataka (15th–16th century)

The ruins of the former kingdom of Vijayanagara, with its capital at Hampi on the Tungabhadra river, tells the story of one of the great empires in Southern India. Here one finds an entire city with ruins of palaces, temples and tanks set in a spectacular natural setting.

| 2500 BC | 2000 BC | 1500 BC | 1000 BC | 500 BC |

As temples became the focus of the everyday life of people, they developed into huge complexes and even cities. Within the many temple walls, the entire town was organized into different sections: the market place leading to the temple where flowers and offerings were sold, homes for the Brahmins, schools, merchants' houses and workshops where craftsmen worked.

Temple Expansion

Temples, especially in South India, expanded into several halls and shrines, huge gateways, tanks, stores and kitchens. Additional mandapas or halls were added for various rituals and activities: a bhog mandapa for feeding pilgrims, a kalyana mandap for weddings, a nat mandap for dance, as well as mandaps for music to entertain the gods and their devotees.

Drawing of a South Indian temple complex

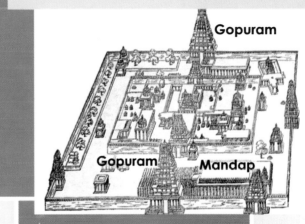

Gopuram

Gopuram   Mandap

Gopuram, Nataraja Temple, Chidambaram, Tamil Nadu

Village fair near a temple town

Gateway to God

Each temple had one or more great gopurams or gateways facing the cardinal directions — north, south, east and west. The gopurams were tall, towering and covered with sculpture so that pilgrims could see them from a distance. As the brick and stone gopurams grew taller, the shikhara over the garbha griha became smaller and were often covered with precious gold.

How do we protect our beautiful temple towns from being destroyed due to haphazard building and encroachments? Is sustainable development the answer?

53

1336- 565 AD, Reign of the Vijaynagar Kings, Hampi

1044-70 AD, Rise of the Cholas in the South
1010 AD, Brihadeshwar temple, Thanjavur

1000-600 BC, The three later Vedas are composed

500 BC   0   500 AD   1000 AD   1500 AD   2000 AD

Seeking Divine Blessing

People go to the temple for darshan or to seek divine blessings and to make offerings of water, flowers, fruits and incense. The main deity in the garbha griha is never moved (achala) and is worshipped throughout the year. The image is bathed each morning, dressed in fine clothes and jewels, and then gifted with garlands of sweet smelling flowers and leaves. At night, the god is put to sleep with music and prayers and the curtain of the garbha griha is drawn.

Adoration of Shiva with garlands

Taking God to the Streets

For each festival associated with a god, like Shivaratri for Shiva or Janmashtami for Krishna, special clothes are put on the murti (deity) and elaborate pujas are performed. At the time of such festivals, murtis made of bronze are taken out in decorated raths or chariots. These wooden raths roll through the streets around the temple so that people can receive a special blessing.

Celebrating the marriage of Shiva, Matangeshvar Temple, Khajuraho, M.P.

Temple Crafts

Kanchipuram, Tamil Nadu, and Varanasi in Uttar Pradesh became famous for their exquisitely woven silk saris. The most sought after saris for generations continue to be woven. The saris are priced according to their weight, taking into consideration the substance of the silk and the extent of the gold thread. A unique system of weavers' co-operatives also makes and sells Kanchi saris.

2500 BC   2000 BC   1500 BC   1000 BC   500 BC

Temple towns became famous pilgrimage centres, also well known for their crafts. These crafts such as textiles and metal images are very popular with pilgrims and visitors.

Bronze image of Nataraja (Shiva, the Lord of Dance), 12th Century, Chola period

Bronze Images
Thanjavur is still famous world over for its bronze images — a tradition that reached its height during the reign of the Chola dynasty (9th-13th) centuries.

The Lost Wax Process
The Dancing Girl from Harappan Civilization was made with the lost wax process (cire per due). The image is first made in wax in exact proportions and then covered in a mould of mud. The wax is melted and runs out of a hole at the bottom of the mould. Molten metal is poured into it, and when cooled, it is released from the mould. This technique allows the metal image to capture the soft sensitivity of wax before it is 'lost' and replaced with hard shiny metal.

Devi, detail of Chola Bronze, 11th century

55

c. 1100 AD, Chola artists used Cire Per Due process

| 500 BC | 0 | 500 AD | 1000 AD | 1500 AD | 2000 AD |

A Place for Prayer
Masjid (mosque) means a place to prostrate in prayer.

A **dome** is a hemispherical roof. A dome is made up of arches to cover a large area.

A **minaret** is the tower from where the muezzin calls people to prayer. This call, or the aazan, is announced five times a day. When the call is heard, the faithful go to the masjid, or pray at home.

The **mihrab** is a decorated niche built in the direction of prayer, facing the holy city of Mecca.

An open **courtyard** provides people space to pray together. Id-gah is a wide open space where thousands gather for Id prayers.

A **tank** is provided for people to wash their hands and face before prayer.

Jama Masjid, Delhi

Jama Masjid
Large mosques or Jama Masjids accommodate thousands of people for the Friday (Jumma) prayer. The courtyard of the Jama Masjid in Delhi can accommodate over 20,000 people.

Islam means submission to the will of Allah. Assalama means to enter in peace. When Arab traders came to India, Islam was introduced into the country. The religion teaches that there is only one god, and his messenger or prophet is Mohammed.

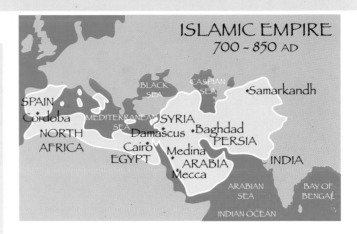

Birth of the Prophet

In the year 570 AD, Mohammed was born in Mecca in Saudi Arabia. At the age of 40, he received God's message that is recorded in the Quran, the source of Islamic law and teaching. Mohammed lived in an unequal society of slaves and masters. He began spreading Allah's message among the people, but many were against him and he had to flee (hijira) from Mecca to Medina. Mohammed later returned to Mecca with his followers to teach people about equality, unity and how to lead peaceful lives.

Festivals

Id-ul-Fitr or Feast of the Breaking Fast is a festival that celebrates the end of Ramzan, when Muslims fast for a month from sunrise to sunset.

Bakrid is the festival that commemorates the great sacrifice of Prophet Ibrahim who was so devoted to God's will that he unhesitatingly agreed to sacrifice his only son Ismail. God was so pleased with his loyalty, that he asked Ibrahim to sacrifice a goat (bakra) instead.

The Qutb Minar

The first stone masjid in Delhi has the famous Qutb Minar built by Qutb-ud-din Aibak in 1199. The minar or tower is 239 feet in height and it is the tallest stone tower in India. The Qutb Minar, Delhi's most popular landmark is a World Heritage Site.

World Heritage Site

12th Century AD, Advent of Islam

1191 AD, Construction of Qutb Minar, New Delhi

500 BC   0   500 AD   1000 AD   1500 AD   2000 AD

The Tomb

In India, the memory of kings, queens, saints and poets as well great personalities in history has been immortalized in magnificent maqbaras or tombs. Near the maqbarahs, masjids and rest houses were also built for pilgrims. Today, annual feasts and festivals such as the Urs commemorating the death anniversary of saints, and other events are also held at tomb sites.

How the shape of the tomb has evolved over the years

Tomb of Ghiyas-ud-din Tughlaq, 14th Century, New Delhi

Lodi Tomb, 15th century, New Delhi

| 2500 BC | 2000 BC | 1500 BC | 1000 BC | 500 BC |

Throughout the Islamic world, the dead are buried in maqbarahs or tombs. Hence royal tombs were set in splendid gardens with water channels. According to Islamic belief, when the world comes to an end, those who have led a good life will go to paradise. The Quran describes paradise as a beautiful and peaceful place where the river of life flows, and there are flowering trees in full bloom.

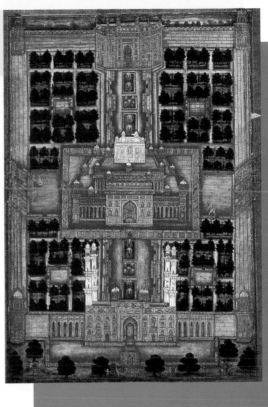

Painting of Mughal garden, Akbar's tomb, 17th Century, Sikandra, near Agra, U.P.

World Heritage Site

Humayun's Tomb, 16th century, New Delhi

World Heritage Site

Taj Mahal, 17th century, Agra, U.P.

Early domes were large and bulbous. The dome in later years became more onion shaped.

1569 AD, Humayun's tomb, New Delhi

1526 AD, Mughal rule begins
1451-1526 AD, Lodis rule Delhi
1320-1414 AD, Tughlaqs rule Delhi

1652 AD, Taj Mahal, Agra

500 BC   0   500 AD   1000 AD   1500 AD   2000 AD

Jali

A pierced window screen made of a single slab of marble or stone. A jali helps in air circulation and also allows the hot afternoon sun to filter in gently. A jali provides privacy too — you can look out but nobody can see what is inside.

Marble jali or screen, Fatehpur Sikri, near Agra, U.P.

Calligraphy

Calligraphy is the art of decorative writing. The word has its origins in the Greek words — kallos (beauty) and graphos (writing). The calligraphy in Islamic architecture are verses from the Quran. On right, calligraphy on Qutb Minar, New Delhi.

Detail of inlay work, Akbar's tomb, Sikandra, near Agra, U.P.

Inlay Work

Inlay work or pietra dura is the technique of placing cut and shaped semi-precious stones into surfaces such as marble to create various patterns. The finest examples can be seen at the Taj Mahal where over 65 separate coloured stones were used to form one flower.

Detail of inlay work, Taj Mahal, Agra, U.P.

2500 BC   2000 BC   1500 BC   1000 BC   500 BC

Islamic buildings are not decorated with images or sculptures, but instead have jalis, inlay work, floral patters, geometric shapes, designs and other architectural features.

Arch

An engineering principle designed by the Romans to carry the weight of the roof and form wide bridges. In Hindu architecture, the weight of the roof fell on the beam. The size of the beam between two pillars could not be too large, as it would crack in the middle. In Islamic architecture in India, both the **beam** and the **arch** were used to create a unique style later called Indo-Islamic.

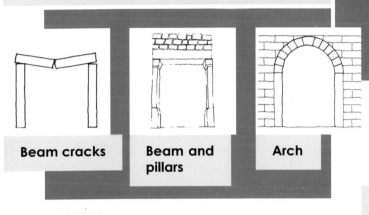

Beam cracks **Beam and pillars** **Arch**

Dome

A dome is formed by joining many arches together over a central square room. The gumbaz or dome or hemispherical roof is a striking feature of Islamic architecture.

Dome of Humayun's Tomb

Humayun's tomb is very special as it has a double dome. The roof seen outside is tall and proportionate with the external view of the building. Inside the main hall, where the tomb of Humayun lies, there is another ceiling that is lower and proportionate to the interior view of the hall. This is why it is known as a double dome.

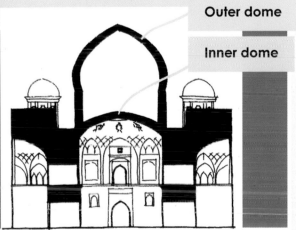

Outer dome

Inner dome

Dome of the Taj Mahal, Agra, U.P.

1571 AD, Mughal Emperor Akbar builds Fatehpur Sikri, near Agra

500 BC   0   500 AD   1000 AD   1500 AD   2000 AD

1526
Babur, the first Mughal emperor invades India from Afghanistan and founds the Mughal Empire on the ruins of the Delhi Sultanate.

1530
Humayun becomes king after the death of Babur, his father.

1556
Akbar, Humayun's son, takes over the throne.

Mughal garden: Babur introduced this style of garden to India

Humayun's Tomb, New Delhi

Akbar's Tomb, Sikandra, near Agra, U.P.

Purana Quila, New Delhi

Royal apartments, Fatehpur Sikri, near Agra, U.P.

2500 BC   2000 BC   1500 BC   1000 BC   500 BC

The rule of the great Mughals (1526-1857) was an exciting period for the arts. Architecture, painting, textiles and jewellery flourished under their patronage. Local artistic traditions, as well as influences from abroad, including Persian and Chinese, resulted in the development of a very special Mughal style.

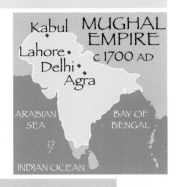

Kabul
Lahore
Delhi
Agra

MUGHAL EMPIRE
c 1700 AD

ARABIAN SEA

BAY OF BENGAL

INDIAN OCEAN

1605
Jehangir succeeds Akbar, his father.

1627
Shah Jahan, the son of Jehangir, becomes emperor.

1659
After a bloody war of succession Aurangzeb becomes the emperor. Following his death in 1707, the dynasty begins to decline.

Jahangir weighing his son in gold

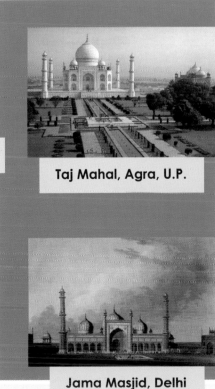

Taj Mahal, Agra, U.P.

Badshahi Mosque, Lahore, Pakistan

Minaret, Jehangir's tomb, Lahore, Pakistan

Jama Masjid, Delhi

1857 AD, Last Mughal Emperor, Bahadur Shah II is dethroned by the British
1639 AD, Red Fort is commissioned by Shah Jahan, Old Delhi
1656 AD, Jama Masjid, Old Delhi
1529 AD, Babur finishes his memoir, the Baburnama

500 BC   0   500 AD   1000 AD   1500 AD   2000 AD

The Harappan Script
The script from the Harappan Civilization is the earliest form of writing in India that we know. This script has still not been deciphered, but when it is, we will learn much more about this civilization that started 5,000 years ago.

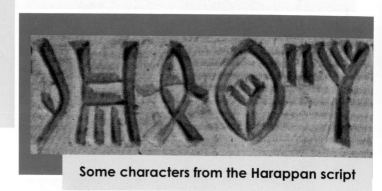

Some characters from the Harappan script

Inscribing History in Stone
Emperor Ashoka instructed the people of his empire on how to lead a good life through inscriptions carved on rocks and pillars. The text was written in the Brahmi script, which is the origin of many scripts in India. Later kings inscribed orders on metal sheets so that it would last for a long time.

Ashokan inscription, Napti Talai, M.P.

Palm leaf manuscript, 18th Century, Orissa

Palm Leaf Manuscripts
Buddhists, Jains and Hindus created religious texts and manuscripts using the palm leaf. The palm tree leaf was dried, and the text was written on the leaf with a reed pen or a metal stylus. The metal stylus created thin grooves on the leaf that was rubbed with charcoal powder so that the letters stood out in black. The page was sometimes painted with illustrations. The leaves were strung together with a sutra or nadi (cord or string) and protected by a pair of wooden covers that were also painted with natural colours.

India has an extraordinary memory. Much of our history, scientific knowledge, mathematics, rhymes, riddles and legends are memorized and passed down from one generation to the next. The story of writing is also an ancient art, and we used many different types of materials to record our knowledge.

Elegant Handwriting

There are many styles of calligraphy of different scripts that developed with the making of the book. The Quran was copied on the finest paper, and decorated with gold and coloured motifs and borders. The Guru Granth Sahib and the Bible were also copied by hand. These hand-written and illustrated masterpieces are treasured in museums around the world.

History of Paper

Paper was invented in China in the 1st century AD. and brought to India by Arab traders in the 10th century AD. Paper is made from the fine pulp of wood, bamboo and cloth, that is dried and laid out in sheets. Books of paper were written by hand and often illustrated by famous artists. It often took several months and years to write a book, and that is why they were extremely precious and valuable and were given as gifts by kings and nobles to their family members on special occasions.

Art of the Book Today

The first printing press was invented in Europe in the 1450s. In India, the first printing was done in Goa. The machine was later imported into Mumbai in 1670. Books are now mass printed, and designing books has become a highly skilled art form. India is the world's third largest producer of English books.

Page from The Quran, Deccan region, 16th Century

Currency note with National languages

65

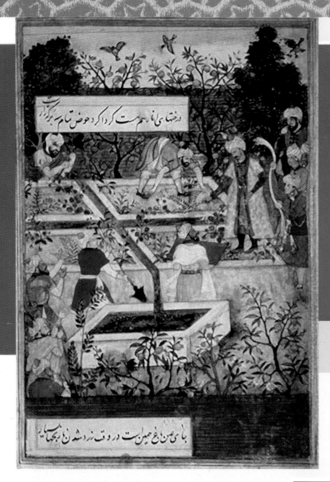

Babar

Babar founded the Mughal Empire in 1526. **Babur-Nama,** his memoirs recorded his daily life, travels, wars and the strange and wonderful things he saw. Humayun, Babur's son, spent many years in exile in the Persian court and was influenced by the architecture, painting and other art forms that he saw there.

Babur supervising the laying out of a garden

Akbar

Akbar came to the throne when he was 13 years old, and though he did not know how to read and write, he loved illustrated books that told the story with the help of paintings. He commissioned the illustration of a text called the **Razm-Nama** — the Persian translation of the Mahabharata that took six years to complete. Akbar also had the history of his ancestors written down with a large number of illustrations, such as the **Timur-Nama** and the **Babur-Nama.** The emperor's own biography, the **Akbar-Nama** was written by his advisor and friend, Abul Fazl.

Akbar amongst wild animals

2500 BC   2000 BC   1500 BC   1000 BC   500 BC

The Mughal emperors commissioned artists for their palace workshops to prepare beautifully illustrated manuscripts and paintings depicting events of their lives, wars, palace festivities, court scenes as well as the natural world.

Jehangir

Akbar's son Jehangir loved miniature or small book-sized paintings. A large number of portraits and illustrations of historic events were painted during his reign. Famous artists like Ustad Mansur created detailed drawings of natural beauty — animals, birds and unusual plants and flowers.

Emperor Jehangir playing Holi

Camel Fight, Jehangir period, Maharashtra

16th Century AD, Humayun invites Persian artists to India

1590 AD, Abu Fazl writes the *Akbar-Nama*

1680 AD, Aurangzeb dismisses painters from his court

500 BC   0   500 AD   1000 AD   1500 AD   2000 AD

How the Painting was Done

Several sheets of good quality paper (Daulatabadi or Irani) were stuck together and the top layer was polished with a smooth agate stone till the surface was perfect. Then the outline was sketched with Indian red colour without glue. Corrections, and the final outline were made with lamp black. The whole paper was then covered with a layer of white and the colours were applied. Borders were often traced using an outline made with perforated holes through which charcoal powder was sprayed on to the paper below.

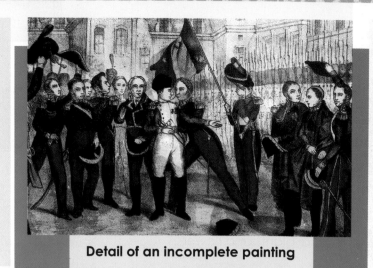

Detail of an incomplete painting

Detail of a border of a miniature painting

A Very Special Skill

Often many artists worked on one painting. One artist specialized in making borders, another did portraits, and younger artists learnt the art of painting by filling in the background colour of their masters' paintings.

Paint

Paint was prepared from more than 25 different pigments. Some paint came from minerals such as multani mitti, and others from plants like henna. Gum Arabic, sugar or linseed oil were used to bind (stick) the colours on to the paper. Illustrations for books were small in size, and required fine brushes made of squirrel tail or camel hair, to achieve delicate details.

Hindola Raga, 17th century

2500 BC   2000 BC   1500 BC   1000 BC   500 BC

Different styles of painting existed throughout the country. When the Mughal Empire began to disintegrate, its artists moved to other kingdoms looking for work, and this led to the development of several schools or styles of Indian painting depicting favourite themes and stories of the royal patrons.

Krishna and Radha celebrating Holi, Kangra School, 18th Century

> *Artists from Basohli used beetle wings for their shimmering greenish-violet colour to depict jewellery in paintings.*

Radha and Krishna, detail of a painting from the Basohli School, 18th century

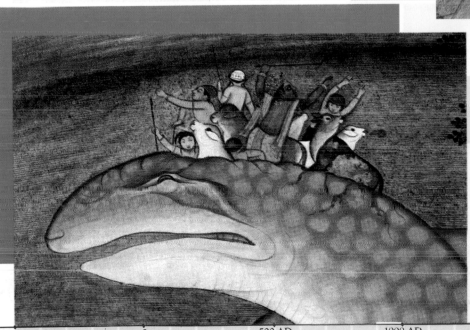

Krishna saving the Gopies from the demon python, Pahari School, 18th Century

c.1560-1850 AD, Deccani Painting flourishes

c.1660-1850 AD, Basohli School

c.1720-1850 AD, Kishangarh School

c.1760-1850 AD, Kangra School

500 BC   0   500 AD   1000 AD   1500 AD   2000 AD

33   The Great Gurus

The ten Sikh Gurus

Life of Guru Nanak

Guru Nanak was born into a Hindu family in Talwandi (now called Nankana Sahib) in Pakistan. He was very inquisitive when he was young. He married and had two sons, and worked as a storekeeper for several years. When he received his spiritual calling or message, he left his work and began travelling to important religious centres of his time.

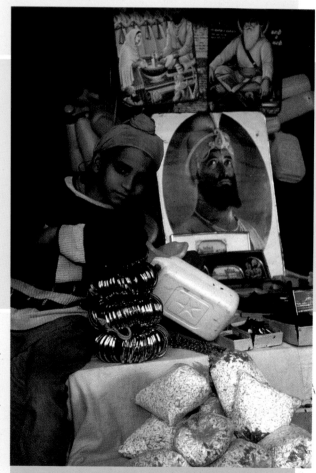

A shop selling religious objects outside the Golden Temple, Amritsar, Punjab

Teachings

"Who can be called bad, who can be called good? For we see the same God within all."

Guru Nanak

Guru Nanak believed in the brotherhood of all people.

Sikh Identity

In the 17th century, the Mughal Emperor Aurangzeb was not tolerant of the Sikh faith. In response to religious oppression, the tenth Guru, Gobind Singh, established the Khalsa — brotherhood of saint-soldiers that were prepared to lay down their lives for the Sikh cause. The Guru gave Sikh men and women a distinctive appearance with the 5 K's:

1. Kesh: hair that must never be cut
2. Kanga: comb
3. Kara: bangle
4. Kaccha: short trousers or underpants
5. Kirpan: small sword

Sikhism, founded by Guru Nanak (1469–1538), is one of the youngest religions of the world. This faith began in Punjab, in the region that once covered areas in India and Pakistan. Guru Nanak was followed by nine gurus, who like him, taught followers to be hardworking and compassionate to one another.

The Guru Granth Sahib

The Guru Granth Sahib or the holy book is regarded as the last Guru — the ultimate spiritual authority for the Sikhs. It contains the teachings of the Gurus as well as verses of Muslim and Hindu saints like Kabir and Namdev. The sacred book was first compiled by the fifth Guru, Arjan Dev, in 1604, and consists of over 1,430 pages in the Gurmukhi script.

Reading of the Guru Granth Sahib, Golden Temple, Amritsar, Punjab

Kar Sevaks at work in a Gurdwara kitchen

Kar Seva is the voluntary contribution of physical labour needed for any kind of work in the Gurudwara. On March 26, 2004, thousands of people volunteered to clean the sacred tank of the Golden Temple. The kar seva was held after 31 years.

Emperor Akbar sharing a meal with his nobles during his visit to Guru Ram Dass

1469 AD, Guru Nanak is born
1606 AD, Jehangir orders execution of Guru Arjan Dev
1699 AD, Guru Gobind Singh forms the Khalsa

500 BC   0   500 AD   1000 AD   1500 AD   2000 AD

Worship of the Guru Granth Sahib, Golden Temple, Amritsar

Paying Respect

People remove their shoes, cover their heads and perform a pradakshina or circumambulation of the tank after bathing. Then they enter the Gurudwara to pay their respects to the Guru Granth Sahib, kept on a raised platform, under a decorated canopy studded with jewels.

Pilgrims walking along the causeway to the Golden Temple

The Golden Temple lit during Diwali

Place for Celebration and Shelter

The Gurudwara is also a place for marriages, celebration of festivals as well as for education and shelter for the poor. Festivals like Baisakhi celebrate the beginning of the harvest of the winter crop, and the New Year. Holi marks the first day of summer, and is celebrated with music and the vigorous Bhangra dance.

Gurupurabs are festivals that commemorate the Gurus. The birthday of Guru Nanak on Kartik Purnima or the full moon night in the month of November is celebrated in Gurudwaras throughout the world.

2500 BC   2000 BC   1500 BC   1000 BC   500 BC

The Gurudwara is the house of the Guru, where the sacred Guru Granth Sahib is kept. Several Gurudwaras were built across the country to mark a special event, such as Nankana Sahib in Pakistan, built to commemorate Guru Nanak's place of birth.

The Golden Temple, Amritsar, Punjab

Harmandir Sahib

The Harmandir Sahib or Golden Temple in Amritsar is the most sacred place for the Sikh community. This beautiful building is enclosed by walls with four gateways opening to all four directions — north, south, east and west, to welcome people of all faiths. The central tank or Amrit Sagar (sea of immortality) is where people bathe and wash before prayer. In the centre of the tank is the Gurudwara, a jewel-like golden clad shrine approached by a pathway.

Ornamentation and Design

The design of the Gurudwara has been influenced by other religious buildings. Its beautiful golden dome is Islamic, while the lotus design and decorations are from Hindu temples. The Maharaja of Punjab, Ranjit Singh, invited artists and painters to embellish the Golden Temple with gold panels, inlay and floral carvings. Inside this golden domed building is the central hall where the Guru Granth Sahib is placed each day. Musical recitation of the Guru Granth Sahib by the Granthi fills the hall where people gather for prayer.

Painted ceiling, Golden Temple, Amritsar

In Service for All

Guru ka langar is the free kitchen attached to the Gurudwara where people of all classes sit and eat together, strengthening the bonds of brotherhood and equality.

1799 AD, Ranjit Singh emerges as the Sikh's most powerful ruler

1588 AD, Guru Arjan Dev builds Harmandir Sahib, Amritsar

500 BC   0   500 AD   1000 AD   1500 AD   2000 AD

Jaisalmer Fort, Rajasthan
The Jaisalmer Fort, in the heart of the Thar desert, is more than 800 years old. It is one of India's oldest living forts.

Red Fort, Delhi
The Mughal emperor, Shah Jahan, built this impressive fort on the west bank of the river Yamuna.

Gwalior Fort, Madhya Pradesh
The Gwalior Fort is one of India's most ancient forts and palaces. It is located on an elevated sandstone hill.

Vijaydurg Fort, Maharashtra
Located on the western coast, this 17th-century fort was a naval base for the Maratha rulers.

Golconda Fort, Andhra Pradesh
It is at this fort that one can capture the splendour of the 16th-century kingdoms of the Deccan.

2500 BC   2000 BC   1500 BC   1000 BC   500 BC

Ancient texts laid down specific guidelines on how and where to build forts. A fort was built for the protection of a settlement against enemy attacks and wild animals. Forts were also used as residences for royal families. Sometimes, entire towns developed within the walls of a fort.

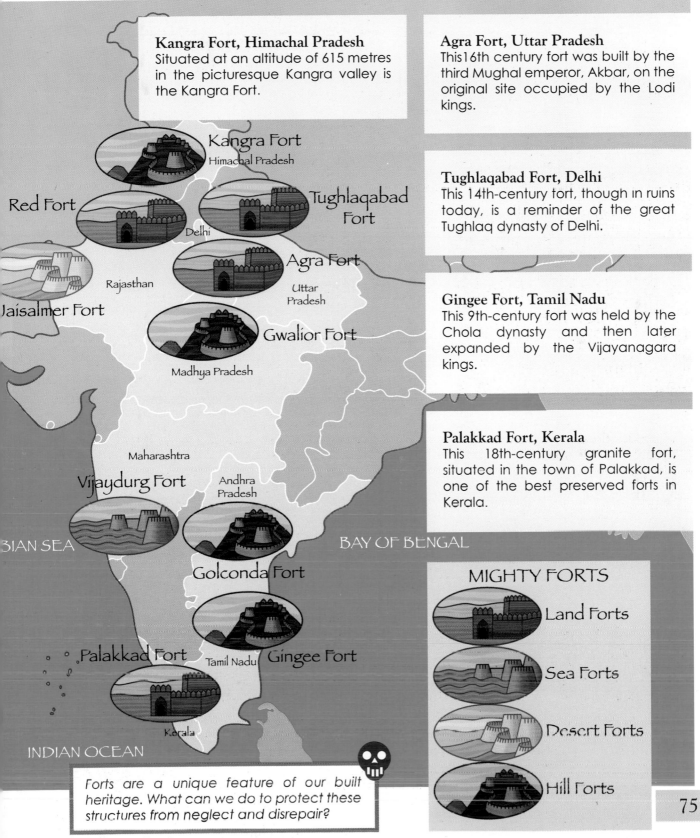

Kangra Fort, Himachal Pradesh
Situated at an altitude of 615 metres in the picturesque Kangra valley is the Kangra Fort.

Agra Fort, Uttar Pradesh
This 16th century fort was built by the third Mughal emperor, Akbar, on the original site occupied by the Lodi kings.

Tughlaqabad Fort, Delhi
This 14th-century fort, though in ruins today, is a reminder of the great Tughlaq dynasty of Delhi.

Gingee Fort, Tamil Nadu
This 9th-century fort was held by the Chola dynasty and then later expanded by the Vijayanagara kings.

Palakkad Fort, Kerala
This 18th-century granite fort, situated in the town of Palakkad, is one of the best preserved forts in Kerala.

Kangra Fort
Himachal Pradesh

Red Fort

Delhi

Tughlaqabad Fort

Rajasthan

Jaisalmer Fort

Agra Fort
Uttar Pradesh

Gwalior Fort
Madhya Pradesh

Maharashtra

Vijaydurg Fort

Andhra Pradesh

ARABIAN SEA

BAY OF BENGAL

Golconda Fort

Palakkad Fort
Tamil Nadu

Gingee Fort

Kerala

INDIAN OCEAN

MIGHTY FORTS

Land Forts

Sea Forts

Desert Forts

Hill Forts

Forts are a unique feature of our built heritage. What can we do to protect these structures from neglect and disrepair?

1751 AD, Emergence of the Marathas — great fort builders

500 BC   0   500 AD   1000 AD   1500 AD   2000 AD

75

FEATURES OF A STRONG FORT

Solid and high **walls** so that the enemy cannot climb into the fort.

A **moat** full of water, surrounding the fort so that the enemy cannot climb the walls easily. Crocodiles in the water to eat up the enemy!

A **gate** that has solid doors, preferably with spikes so that elephants cannot knock it down.

A **slit** above the gate so that hot oil can be poured on the enemy entering the fort.

Safe **underground passages** for escape.

A safe **treasury** to hide the treasures of the kingdom.

Forts were built to protect royal palaces and their treasuries. Early forts were made of mud but later acquired their imposing and intimidating appearance when huge stone fortifications and gates were built around the royal city.

Strategic Places to Build a Fort
• On a hilltop, so you can see the approaching enemy attack
• Beside a river or water source, so that while the enemy is struggling to cross the river there is time to attack them
• On the coast or seashore, because the enemy can be spotted far out in the open sea

Thin **openings** on the walls of the fort so that soldiers can shoot the enemy without getting hurt.

Comfortable **palaces** for the royal family, **places of worship** and **barracks** for soldiers, staff, and **stables** for elephants and horses.

Huge **storage tanks** for water, and granaries for food inside the fort so that if it is surrounded, people can continue to live for years, without having to surrender.

Shish Mahal, Amber Fort, Jaipur, Rajasthan

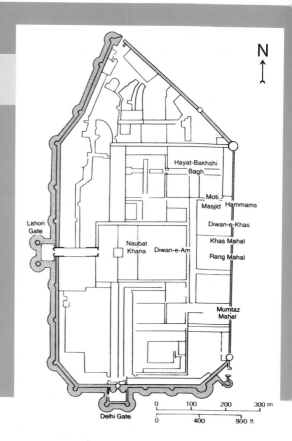

Plan of Red Fort, Old Delhi

Shish Mahal

The ceiling was decorated with thousands of mirrors that reflected the oil lamps below, making the Shish Mahal glimmer like the night sky full of stars. Here the king would entertain his family and friends to music and discourses.

Maidan or Parade Grounds

Maidans were used for festivities, elephant and camel fights, for sporting events and parades.

Diwan-i-Am, Red Fort, Old Delhi

Diwan-i-Am

The Diwan-i-Am was the hall of public audience where royal visitors and ambassadors would gather to meet the king on designated days and times, and present gifts and ask for requests. Ordinary citizens rarely came before the emperor, except for judgement and execution!

2500 BC   2000 BC   1500 BC   1000 BC   500 BC

Indian royalty built palaces of unique style and beauty. In the palace, there was a clear demarcation of private and public spaces. There were often special areas for women, to entertain guests, and for the king and his activities.

Diwan-i-Khas
The Diwan-i-Khas was the hall of private audience of the emperor with his family.

Luxury Baths
The palace had hammams for bath ing. Water heated over wood fires would be transported through pipes into indoor water pools and tanks.

Diwan-i-Khas, City Palace, Jaipur, Rajasthan

Interior of Meherangarh Fort, Jodhpur, Rajasthan

Interiors
From paintings we know that palace interiors did not have much furniture, but luxurious carpets, bolsters, cush-ions and screens. Depending on the weather, the royal residents spent time outside, enjoying the winter sunshine and warmth, or inside, away from the heat of the day. Within the palace, open courtyards and private gardens were used for play, entertainment and celebra-tion of festivals.

Painting of City Palace, Jaipur, Rajasthan

Prince and Princess, Chowmahalla Palace, Hyderabad

1900 AD, City Palace, Jaipur
1639 AD, Red Fort, Old Delhi
1592 AD, Amber Fort, Jaipur
1499 AD Meherangarh Fort, Jodhpur

500 BC   0   500 AD   1000 AD   1500 AD   2000 AD

38   Traders Come to Stay

Fort William, Calcutta (Kolkata)

Fort William is one of the most impressive buildings of British India, and it still continues to serve as a citadel of the Indian army. There were actually two Fort Williams, the old and the new. The old fort goes back to the early days of the East India Company. Sir Charles Eyre started the first construction of the fort, and his successor, John Beard, added other parts to the structure. On completion in 1702, the fort was named after King William of England.

Trading Posts

During this time, the traders did not bring their families to India, so the buildings that were built were functional such as warehouses, ice factories, forts and military barracks, housing for soldiers and other buildings for the purposes of government and the church.

Residency, Lucknow, U.P.

Writers' Building, Calcutta (Kolkata)

The building was built between 1776 and 1780 to house junior officers of the East India Company. One of the most imposing public buildings constructed during this period, the Writers' Building today serves as the administrative centre for the state of West Bengal. The Chief Minister's office is also located in this building.

Fort St. George, Madras (Chennai)

Fort St. George was the home of the military garrison. It houses the Church of St. Mary (1678-1680), one of the oldest churches in India. Today, the building is the office of the State Legislature of Tamil Nadu. It has an interesting museum of documents and paintings of this period.

| 2500 BC | 2000 BC | 1500 BC | 1000 BC | 500 BC |

It was during the Mughal rule in the 16th century that European merchants and ambassadors began visiting the sub-continent to establish trade contacts. The Portuguese settled in Goa and Kerala, the French in the south and the British in Surat, Bombay, Calcutta and Madras. Royal permission was given to foreign investors to set up trading posts and warehouses to store goods for export to Europe.

Shift of Power

While the Mughal Dynasty was losing power, the British East India Company was taking over different parts of India through its trade deals. With the defeat of Tipu Sultan of Mysore in 1799, the British became the most powerful political and military force in India.

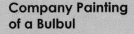

Company Painting of a Bulbul

Company Paintings

The British established the East India Company for trade purposes. The company in the late 18th-19th centuries employed artists to depict various aspects of India: people, everyday life and natural history. These works were known as Company Paintings.

Panna Palace, Panna, M.P.

Inspiration Europe

European influence on the arts of India can be seen in the architecture of royal palaces and fashions of Indian royalty. Indian palaces of this period were filled with both good and poor quality art objects bought from Europe.

Churches of Goa

In the 16th century, when the Portuguese brought priests from Portugal to India, churches, full of gold ornamentation and painted statues were built in Goa. One of the churches, the Basilica of Bom Jesus, contains the sacred body of St. Francis Xavier, a pioneering Christian missionary who worked in Asia in the 16th century. Every 10 years, on the anniversary of the Saint's death, the holy relics of the Saint are displayed for public viewing.

Basilica of Bom Jesus, Goa

Casket containing the relics of St. Francis Xavier, Goa

World Heritage Site

1600 AD, British East India Co. is founded
1510 AD, Portuguese occupy Goa | 1761 AD,
1498 AD, Portuguese explorer, Vasco Da Gama, | St. Thomas, Calcutta's
discovers sea route from Europe to India | first church is built

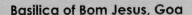
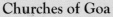

500 BC   0   500 AD   1000 AD   1500 AD   2000 AD

The Good Life

As time went on and the British were firmly established in India, they brought their families from England. British women introduced their style of living, knowledge of flowers, latest fashions and art from England into their lives in India, so that they would not miss home.

British Bungalows

The British generally lived in spacious bungalows and had a large staff to run the household.

Victoria Memorial, Calcutta (Kolkata)

On the death of Queen Victoria in January 1901, Lord Curzon, who was then the Viceroy of India, suggested the building of the Victoria Memorial. Today, the Memorial has in its possession, a wonderful collection of photographs, maps, paintings and sculptures from the British period, as well as a permanent exhibition on the history of Kolkata.

2500 BC   2000 BC   1500 BC   1000 BC   500 BC

After 1857 and the rebellion that followed, the British decided to take administrative control of Indian territory, and great buildings were built in Madras, Calcutta and Bombay and also smaller cities to establish the Empire across the country.

Victoria Terminus, Bombay
(Chhatrapati Shivaji Terminus, Mumbai)

Imposing stations were built, like the Victoria Terminus (V.T.) railway station that was similar to St. Pancras Station in London. An English architect, Fredrick Williams Stevens, built V.T. over a period of 10 years starting in 1878. He built a magnificent building of yellow sandstone and gray granite with high arches and stained-glass windows. The railway station was built to honour Queen Victoria. It was from here that India's first steam engine puffed out to neighbouring Thane, about 45 km away.

Victoria Terminus was declared a World Heritage Site by UNESCO in 2004.

British India's Greatest Gift

A major innovation in transport and technology in India came with the introduction of the railway. Railway lines were laid across India, even in hill stations that were otherwise inaccessible.

World Heritage Site

Fabulous Faces

Victoria Terminus is famous for its carvings of faces of mythical creatures or Gargoyles.

Town Hall, Bombay
(Asiatic Society, Mumbai)

The Town Hall, an elegant building with wonderful columns, was built by the British over 200 years ago. Today, it is known as the Asiatic Society of Mumbai and is a valuable resource for scholars and students, with a library of over 700,000 rare and antique books, and an ancient coin collection.

1857 AD, Indian Mutiny; Universities established in Metro cities ⌐
1853 AD, First rail line between Bombay-Thane opens ⌐
1803 AD, British occupy Delhi ⌐

500 BC   0   500 AD   1000 AD   1500 AD   2000 AD

Dome
In designing the dome of the Viceroy's house, the architect, Lutyens, was inspired by the dome of St. Paul's Cathedral in London, U.K. and the Sanchi Stupa.

Chattri
A chattri is a domed pavilion commonly used in Rajasthani buildings that was also borrowed by Lutyens.

Architectural features, Rashtrapati Bhavan, New Delhi

Chajja
A chajja, a common element in Mughal buildings, is also seen in Lutyens design. Chajjas protect the walls and windows of a building from the hot sun as well as from rain and strong winds.

Love for Geometry
The architects loved using geometric shapes in their plans for the new capital. If you look at the plan of New Delhi, you will notice the use of various geometric shapes such as the hexagon and the triangle.

A **hexagonal system** made up of **triangles** is where all the important public and private buildings were located as well as buildings for commercial purposes.

The **central avenue (rectangle)** known as Kingsway and now called Rajpath. Rajpath was designed as a processional path that linked the Viceroy's House (west) to the War Memorial Arch or India Gate (east).

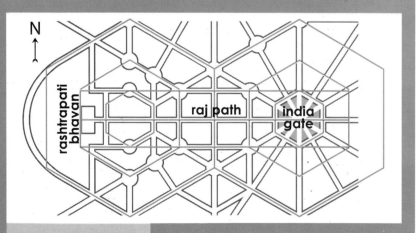

N

rashtrapati bhavan   raj path   india gate

Plan of New Delhi

Do you think the colonial names of our cities should be replaced by new ones?

2500 BC   2000 BC   1500 BC   1000 BC   500 BC

In 1911, Delhi was chosen to be the capital of the British Empire in India, not Calcutta, the London of the East, nor Bombay, the centre of commerce and trade. The announcement of this special news was made by George V, the King of England, at his coronation durbar. The city took 20 years to build, and it was inaugurated in 1931.

The Chosen Ones
Sir Edwin Lutyens and Sir Herbert Baker were the two chief English architects chosen to design and plan Imperial Delhi. They used several motifs and styles from ancient Indian architecture.

Viceroy's House (Rashtrapati Bhavan)
Lutyens designed a home as grand as a palace for the Viceroy, who was to rule on behalf of the King of England. This impressive building is now the Rashtrapati Bhavan where the President of India lives. Built in red and buff sandstone, it has 340 rooms, 227 columns, 37 fountains and a beautiful garden with hundreds of varieties of flowers and plants.

Kingsway (Rajpath)
Today, Rajpath comes alive during Republic Day celebrations held every year on 26th January. An impressive military parade and a colourful procession of school children and mobile tableaux representing different states move down Rajpath passing the President, other dignitaries and cheering crowds.

In Memory
The All India War Memorial Arch, now fondly known as India Gate, was built in memory of 90,000 Indian soldiers who died fighting several wars for the British. An eternal flame, the Amar Jawan Jyoti, in the monument pays homage to the Unknown Soldier.

1933 AD, Connaught Place, New Delhi
1931 AD, New Delhi is inaugurated
1921 AD, India Gate, New Delhi
1913 AD, Lutyens appointed to design Viceroy's house, New Delhi

500 BC   0   500 AD   1000 AD   1500 AD   2000 AD

41 New Materials – New Ideas

Cowasi Jehangir Hall, Bombay (Mumbai)
Built in 1911 and redesigned in 1996
Architect: George Wittet and redesigned by Romi Khosla

The Cowasji Jehangir Hall, originally a part of the Institute of Science, was built in 1911 by a British architect, George Wittet, with a donation of Rs. 400,000 given by Sir Cowasji Jehangir. In 1996, the Hall was converted to a museum of modern art (National Gallery of Modern Art), with wonderful split-level galleries to display paintings and other art objects.

Gateway of India, Bombay (Mumbai)
Built in 1924
Architect: George Wittet

Mumbai's most famous landmark was built on the water's edge to commemorate the visit of King George V and Queen Mary to the city before they attended the Delhi Darbar in 1911. Behind this great arch, there are steps leading down to the water from where visitors can take a cruise around the city's harbour.

Although India has progressed greatly since independence, a lot remains to be done. We still need to provide good roads, clean water, adequate housing and a healthy environment for all Indian citizens.

Indian Institute of Management (IIM), Bangalore
Built in 1973
Architect: Balkrishna Doshi

The 100 acre campus of the institute consists of stone buildings with large spaces and courtyards surrounded by trees and landscaped gardens.

| | 2500 BC | 2000 BC | 1500 BC | 1000 BC | 500 BC |

It was through the Gateway of India that the last British troops left the country in 1947. Since independence, Indian ideas of space and design have changed considerably. New materials like cement, reinforced concrete, glass and steel are used to create new forms of architecture. Our cityscapes have changed forever with the construction of skyscrapers and modern buildings.

Experimenting with the Old and New

There are over 100 schools of architecture in India today, where young architects are trained in modern building techniques. There are also several architects who are experimenting with traditional building materials like brick and mud, and ancient techniques and engineering principles to create a truly contemporary Indian architectural vocabulary that is better suited to our varying climate and our lifestyle.

Jawahar Kala Kendra, Jaipur
Built in 1986-92
Architect: Charles Correa
This building is one of Jaipur's finest examples of modern architecture. It is a vibrant cultural complex with an amphitheatre, a library, art studios, exhibition spaces as well as a centre for the performing arts, craft fairs and film screenings. The Kendra is also well known for its permanent collection of Rajasthani paintings and sculpture.

Bahai Temple, New Delhi
Built in 1986
Architect: Fariborz Sahba, a Canadian architect of Iranian origin
The Bahai Temple is the place of worship for the Bahai sect that originated in Persia. It is an amazing structure in the shape of a white marble lotus with 27 petals surrounded by 9 pools and 27 acres of lawns. It has an auditorium that can seat up to 1,300 people and everyone is welcome to attend the service.

The Center for Development Studies, Tiruvanthapuram, Kerala

Architects from Abroad

Several buildings and even entire cities of India have been designed by architects from different parts of the world.

Le Corbousier	The City of Chandigarh
Joseph Allen Stein	Habitat Centre, New Delhi
Laurie Baker	The Centre for Development Studies, Thiruvananthapuram, Kerala

1980-84 AD, Gandhi Labour Inst., B. Doshi, Ahmedabad
1980-82 AD, Asian Games Village, Raj Rewal, New Delhi
1976 AD, Rock Garden, Nek Chand, Chandigarh
1970-86 AD, Kanchenjunga Apts.,Charles Correa, Mumbai

87

500 BC   0   500 AD   1000 AD   1500 AD   2000 AD

Art Schools

India had several famous art schools and colleges of art. Some were started by the British and others like Shantiniketan in West Bengal were established by eminent citizens of India such as the great philosopher and poet, Rabindranath Tagore.

Roots of Indian Modern Art

The turn of the 1900s saw the development of an influential art movement. Several Bengali intellectuals and artists such as Rabindranath Tagore and his nephew Abanindranath started the Bengal School of Art, to find new expressions for Indian artists and free them from British domination and influence. Jamini Roy (1887-1972) was one of the great artists of this school.

Painting by Amrita Shergil

Detail of painting by Jamini Roy

A Great Influence

Amrita Shergil's (1913-1941) father was from Punjab and her mother was Hungarian. She trained in Paris but chose to paint Indian themes. She died at the age of 29, but her contribution to the Indian art movement is enormous.

Painting by B.C. Sanyal

Painting by R. H. Raza

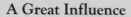

Artists Today

Today, there is a thriving art movement in India. M.F Hussain (born 1914), B.C Sanyal (1902-2003), Francis Souza (1924-2004) and S.H. Raza (born 1922) laid the foundation for future generations of contemporary artists. Their works have become popular among patrons even outside India.

2500 BC	2000 BC	1500 BC	1000 BC	500 BC

After 1947, Indians witnessed dramatic changes in their cultural lives. New mediums and technological innovations have led to the emergence of exciting art forms like cinema, installation art and digital photography that are used by Indian artists to create contemporary and meaningful artworks. Today, Indian art — both ancient and modern, is valued throughout the world.

Eros Cinema, Mumbai, Maharashtra

Cinema Halls

India was one of the first countries in the world to make films. The building of cinema halls began during British rule, in the early 1900s when movie going was a grand spectacle of lavish costumes accompanied by ballroom dances. Cinema halls in Bombay (Mumbai) such as Metro, Eros and Regal, as well as several others in Calcutta (Kolkata) and Madras (Chennai) were constructed in a style known as Art Deco — characterized by geometric designs, bold colours, and the use of plastic and glass.

The First Movies

Telling stories using paintings on cloth or paper, puppets, songs or folklore is an ancient Indian tradition. In 1896, at the Watson Hotel in Bombay (Mumbai), people in India experienced a new and exciting way of telling stories through moving images. They watched their first film, a foreign production by the Lumière Brothers.

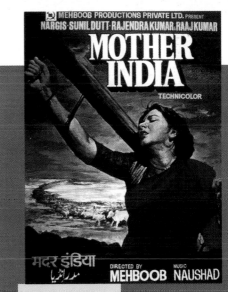

Film poster

India's First Feature Film

In 1913, India's first feature film, Raja Harischandra by Dadasaheb Phalke, was screened for the public. Today, India makes about 800 films a year!

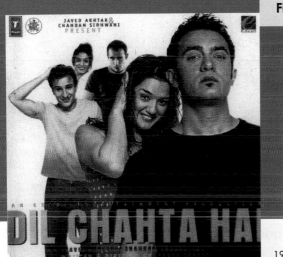

Film poster

Many artists live in poverty today and do not get the recognition they deserve. We need to promote the artistic talents of our national treasures as the reputation of India as a creative land rests on them. We need to encourage young people to study the arts in school so that India continues to remain smart in art.

1975 AD, Hit film, Sholay, released
1957 AD, JJ School of Art established
1947 AD, Progressive Artists' Group formed
1935 AD, Jamini Roy awarded the Viceroy's medal for painting

| 500 BC | 0 | 500 AD | 1000 AD | 1500 AD | 2000 AD |

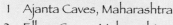

1 Ajanta Caves, Maharashtra
2 Ellora Caves, Maharashtra
3 Agra Fort, Uttar Pradesh
4 Taj Mahal, Uttar Pradesh
5 Sun Temple, Konarak, Orissa
6 Group of Monuments at Mahabalipuram, Tamil Nadu
7 Churches and Convents of Goa, Goa
8 Khajuraho Group of Monuments, Madhya Pradesh
9 Group of Monuments at Hampi, Karnataka
10 Fatehpur Sikri, near Agra, Uttar Pradesh
11 Group of Monuments at Pattadakal, Karnataka
12 Elephanta Caves, near Mumbai, Maharashtra
13 Great Living Chola Temples, Tamil Nadu
14 Buddhist Monuments at Sanchi, Madhya Pradesh
15 Humayun's Tomb, New Delhi
16 Qutb Minar and its Monuments, New Delhi
17 Darjeeling Himalayan Railway (DHR) and the Nilgiri Mountain Railway, West Bengal and Kerala
18 Mahabodhi Temple Complex at Bodh Gaya, Bihar
19 Rock Shelters of Bhimbetka, Madhya Pradesh
20 Champaner-Pavagadh Archaeological Park, Gujarat
21 Chhatrapati Shivaji Terminus (formerly Victoria Terminus), Mumbai, Maharashtra
22 Kaziranga National Park, Assam
23 Manas Wildlife Sanctuary, Assam
24 Keoladeo National Park, Rajasthan
25 Sundarbans National Park, West Bengal
26 Nanda Devi and the Valley of Flowers National Parks, Uttaranchal

The World Heritage Committee of UNESCO nominates over 800 exceptional built and natural sites across the world annually. These World Heritage Sites (WHS) are special because they are of priceless value and need to be protected and conserved by humankind as a whole.

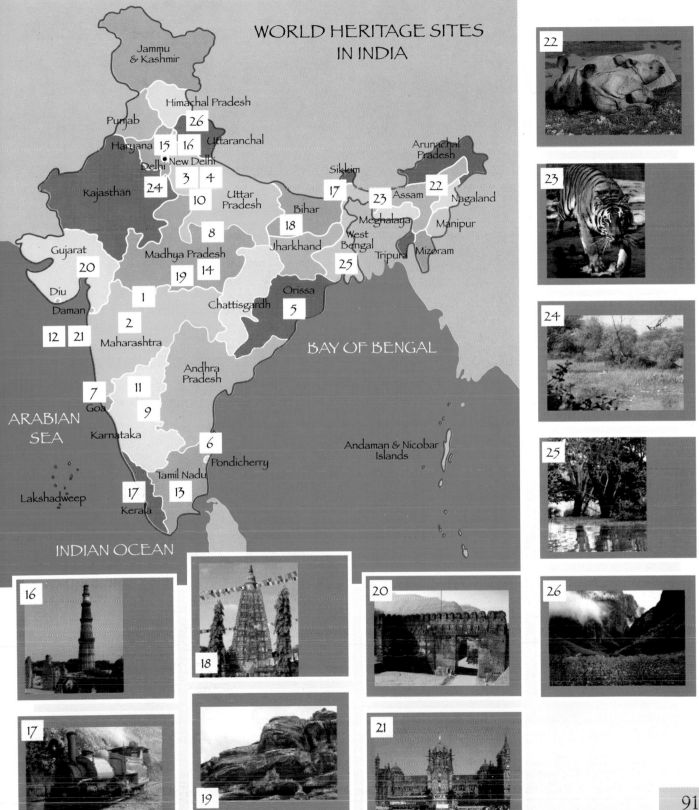

Stop the cutting down of our forests. Plant trees wherever you can.

Stop poaching of wild animals.

Natural Heritage
Mountains, forests, deserts, seas, rivers, lakes, flowers, animals and birds as well as everything that makes up India's non-renewable resources.

Stop the pollution of our rivers and seas.

Living Heritage
Artists such as painters, sculptors, weavers, potters, writers, poets, dancers, singers, musicians and actors.

Grandparents and previous generations who have taught their skills to young people.

We need creative people to help us build a better and more exciting world to live in. A large number of India's artists and craftsmen live in poverty. We must support and nurture their artistic talent.

Our heritage is a precious gift that can never be replaced if it is lost. When you say, "I've inherited my grandfather's pocket watch," it means that your grandfather gifted his precious belonging to you when he passed away, so that you can remember him always. In the same way, when we speak of India's heritage, we mean everything that our country has gifted to us, and all that our ancestors have created.

Stop our historic buildings from being vandalized and destroyed.

Much of India's rich natural, built, living, tangible, intangible heritage is under threat of destruction because of our negligence. It is the fundamental duty of every citizen to preserve & protect our common composite heritage.

Built Heritage
Tombs, forts and palaces, religious buildings, cities, towns and villages.

Historic buildings such as the Red Fort in Delhi give you an idea of how Emperor Shah Jahan lived, the designs he thought beautiful and the skills used to build palaces 400 years ago.

Photographs from your childhood tell you how you looked and behaved when you were young. In the same way old buildings, sculptures and paintings tell the story of India in her younger days, of how people lived in earlier times, the clothes they wore, the type of homes they lived in and other aspects of that time.

Kandarlya Mahadev Temple, Khajuraho, a 19th century image

Kandariya Mahadev Temple, Khajuraho, present day

93

Photo & Drawing Credits

Chapter 1: Centre for Cultural Resources and Training (CCRT), Fredrik Arvidsson (The Guide Book Company Limited, Hong Kong).

Chapter 2: Jean-Louis Nou (The Guide Book Company Limited), National Gallery of Modern Art, New Dellhi, CCRT.

Chapter 3: CCRT, Jean-Louis Nou, Peter Ryan, Norma Joesph, Gerald Cubitt (This is India), Bindu Manchanda (Rajinder Bhandari, Jaisalmer).

Chapter 4: CCRT.

Chapter 5: Anita Sharma, Jean-Louis Nou.

Chapter 6: Gerald Cubitt, Private collection, Kulbhushan and Minakshi Jain (Architecture of the Indian Desert).

Chapter 7: Rajinder Bhandari (Bindu Manchanda), Kulbhushan and Minakshi Jain, Gerald Cubitt, Uzma Mohsin, CCRT.

Chapter 8: Pankaj Shah, Fredrik Arvidsson.

Chapter 9: CCRT, Jean-Louis Nou, Fredrik Arvidsson.

Chapter 10: CCRT, Jean-Louis Nou.

Chapter 11: CCRT, National Museum, Gerald Cubitt.

Chapter 12: CCRT.

Chapter 13: CCRT, Fredrik Arvidsson.

Chapter 14: Jean-Louis Nou, National Museum, New Delhi, Toby Sinclair.

Chapter 15: Fredrik Arvidsson, Jean-Louis Nou, CCRT.

Chapter 16: National Book Trust, Jean-Louis Nou, CCRT.

Chapter 17: Fredrik Arvidsson, CCRT.

Chapter 18: Fredrik Arvidsson.

Chapter 19: CCRT, Tim Harvey.

Chapter 20: Rohini Kandhari.

Chapter 21: CCRT, Fredrik Arvidsson.

Chapter 22: CCRT, Fredrik Arvidsson.

Chapter 23: Kamal Sahai. Gerald Cubitt, CCRT.

Chapter 24: Fredrik Arvidsson, Satish Grover (Roli Books), Kamal Sahai.

Chapter 25: Simon Reddy, Kamal Sahai, Pankaj Shah, Jean-Louis Nou.

Chapter 26: Priya Sen, CCRT.

Chapter 27: CCRT, Toby Sinclair.

Chapter 28: CCRT, Fredrik Arvidsson, Lucy Peck.

Chapter 29: CCRT, Fredrik Arvidsson, Toby Sinclair, National Museum.

Chapter 30: Anita Varma, Jean-Louis Nou, CCRT.

Chapter 31: Rampur Raza Library, Jean-Louis Nou, National Museum.

Chapter 32: Jean-Louis Nou.

Chapter 33: Sondeep Shankar.

Chapter 34: Fredrik Arvidsson, Sondeep Shankar.

Chapter 35: CCRT, Rajinder Bhandari (Bindu Manchanda), Fredrik Arvidsson.

Chapter 36: CCRT.

Chapter 37: Chowmahalla Palace, Jean-Louis Nou, Fredrik Arvidsson.

Chapter 38: Shraman Jha (Jet Wings 'Kolkata'), Private Collection, CCRT, Fredrik Arvidsson.

Chapter 39: Private Collection, Jet wings 'Kolkata'.

Chapter 40: Ram Rahman, Raaj Dayal. Amit Mehra (Aman Nath).

Chapter 41: Private Collection, Fredrik Arvidsson, CCRT.

Chapter 42: Private Collection., INTACH book.

Chapter 43: CCRT, Fredrik Arvidsson, Satish Grover (Roli Books), Neil McAllister, Gerald Cubitt.

Chapter 44: CCRT, Fredrik Arvidsson, Gerald Cubitt.

Bibliography

1. Great Monuments of India, Shobita Punja, The Guide Book Company Limited, Hong Kong, 1994.
2. Khajuraho and its Historic Surroundings, Shobita Punja, Odyssey, Hong Kong, 1994.
3. Museums of India, Shobita Punja, Penguin Books India, 1998.
4. This is India, Shobita Punja, Gerald Cubitt, New Holland Publishers, United Kingdom, 1996.
5. The Golden Temple, The Guide Book Company Limited, Hong Kong, 1992.
6. Orissa, The Guide Book Company Limited, Hong Kong, 1994.
7. Benares, The Guide Book Company Limited, Hong Kong, 1995, 1992.
8. Aurangabad – Culture, Art and Architecture, INTACH Aurangabad Chapter.
9. Japan, Dorling Kindersley.
10. Rampur Raza Library – Monograph, W.H. Siddiqi, Rampur Raza Library, Rampur, 1998.
11. The Book in India, Editor B.S. Kesavan, National Book Trust, India, Delhi, 1992.
12. Alladin and other Tales from the Arabian Nights, Rosalind Kerven, Dorling Kindersley, 1998.
13. Sanskriti, Sanskriti Pratishthan, New Delhi, 2005.
14. Jaisalmer, Bindu Manchanda, HarperCollins Publishers India, New Delhi, 2001.
15. Architecture of the Indian Desert, Kulbhushan and Minakshi Jain, AADI Centre, Ahmedabad, 2000.
16. Masterpieces of Traditional Indian Architecture, Satish Grover, Roli & Janssen BV, New Delhi, 2004.
17. Jet Wings, Kolkata, Vol 5, Issue 12.
18. The Art of India, C. Sivaramamurti, Abrams, New York, 1974.
19. Bombay - The Cities Within, Sharda Dwivedi, India Book House, Bombay, 1995.
20. Hands on Heritage, INTACH, New Delhi, 2003.

Classic books on Indian Culture

1. The Wonder That Was India, A.L. Basham, Rupa & Co, 1994.
2. Handicrafts of India, Kamaladevi Chattopadhyay, ICCR, New Delhi, 1975.
3. History of India and Indonesian Art, Coomaraswamy, Dover, New York, reprint 1985.
4. The Earth Mother: An Introduction to the ritual Arts of Rural India, Pupul Jayakar, Penguin, New Delhi, 1981.
5. Speaking Tree, Richard Lanoy, Oxford University Press, New York, 1971.
6. A History of India, Vol. I, Romilla Thapar, Harmondsworth: Penguin, 1966.
7. A History of India, Vol. II, Percival Spear, Harmondsworth: Penguin, 1966.
8. Classical Indian Dance in Literature and the Arts, Kapila Vatsyayan, Sangeet Natak Akademi, New Delhi, 1977.

National Symbols

Animal – Tiger
Scientific name *Panthera tigris (Linnaeus)*.
The magnificent tiger, Lord of the Jungle, has a thick coat of alternate black and yellow stripes. The Government of India started Project Tiger in 1973 to preserve the endangered tiger population.
Today, the tiger is a symbol of India's wildlife conservation efforts. By saving the tiger we save our forests, water resources and eco-systems.
Symbolism: courage, power, grace, strength.

Anthem – Jana Gana Mana
Original composition is in Bengali by Rabindranath Tagore.
The Constituent Assembly of India adopted the Hindi version as the national anthem, on 24 January 1950.
It was first sung on 27 December 1911 at the Calcutta Session of the Indian National Congress.

Bird – Peacock
Scientific name *Pavo cristatus (Linnaeus)*.
The peacock is the world's most beautiful bird, with a colourful fan-shaped tail. It is protected under the Indian Wildlife (Protection) Act, 1972.
Symbolism: beauty, grace, pride, coming of monsoons.

Flag
India's national flag is a horizontal tricolor with equal bands of saffron, white and green. In the centre of the white band is a navy blue Chakra or wheel with 24 spokes. The ratio of width of the flag to its length is two to three.
Symbolism: Saffron – sacrifice, courage   **White** – peace, truth   **Green** – fertility, growth, good fortune
Wheel – The Dharmachakra of spiritual evolution.

Flower – Lotus
Scientific name *Nelumbo Nucifera*.
The lotus rises out of still, stagnant water to bloom in glorious colours of red, white or pink.
Symbolism: divinity, knowledge, enlightenment, long life.

Fruit – Mango
Botanical Name *Mangifera indica*.
Over 500 varieties are cultivated in India and savoured for their sweet juice rich in vitamin A, C and D. The mango appears in the poems of Kalidasa, memoirs of Alexander and Hieun Tsang, the Chinese pilgrim. Akbar planted 100,000 mango trees in Darbhanga, Bihar.
Symbolism: flowers – springtime and love.

Game - Hockey
The game was introduced in India by the British Army regiments and the first Hockey Club was started in Calcutta in 1885-86.
Major Dhyanchand made hockey popular as a national game. 1928-1956 was the Golden Era of hockey when India won 6 successive gold medals at the Olympic Games.

Song - Vande Mataram
Originally composed in Sanskrit by the Bengali poet Bankim Chandra Chatterji, it became synonymous with the Indian struggle for independence.

Tree – Banyan
Scientific name *Ficus Bengalensis*.
This evergreen, indigenous Indian tree is capable of growing to 30m or taller. The shoots develop roots that grow into new trunks and can cover several acres. The largest, oldest known banyan tree is in Adyar in Chennai, covering an area of 59,500 sq ft. The tree in the Botanical Garden, Calcutta, occupies 1.6 hectares with 100 subsidiary trunks.
Symbolism: referred to as Kalpavriksha or the tree of fulfillment.